Gods, Goddesses, and Mythology

VOLUME 3

Central Asia–Dragons

Marshall Cavendish
New York • London • Singapore

Marshall Cavendish
99 White Plains Road
Tarrytown, New York 10591

www.marshallcavendish.us

© 2005 Marshall Cavendish Corporation

Library of Congress Cataloging-in-Publication Data

Gods, goddesses, and mythology/editor, C. Scott Littleton.
    p. cm.
    Includes bibliographical references and index.
    ISBN 0-7614-7559-1 (set : alk. paper)
1. Mythology--Encyclopedias. I. Littleton, C. Scott. II. Marshall Cavendish Corporation. III. Title.

    BL312.G64 2005
    201'.3'03--dc22

2004040758

ISBN 0-7614-7559-1 (set)
ISBN 0-7614-7562-1 (vol. 3)

Printed and bound in China

09 08 07 06 05   6 5 4 3 2

General Editor
C. Scott Littleton, Occidental College, Los Angeles

Marshall Cavendish
Project Editor: Marian Armstrong
Editorial Director: Paul Bernabeo
Production Manager: Alan Tsai

Brown Reference Group
Project Editor: Chris King
Editors: Sally MacEachern, Henry Russell, Lee Stacy
Designer: Steve Wilson
Picture Researcher: Helen Simm
Cartographer: Mark Walker
Indexer: Kay Ollerenshaw
Managing Editor: Tim Cooke

Picture Credits

CONTENTS

CENTRAL ASIA
AND THE STEPPES

Central Asia and the Steppes comprise a vast tract of land to the north of the Himalayas, to the west of the traditional center of China, and to the east of the Indo-Iranian culture areas of the Middle East. The region has rarely been united as a single political entity, instead consisting mainly of nomadic tribal groups that developed their own cultures and mythologies.

To understand the peoples and cultures of Central Asia and the Steppes, it is essential to understand their history and the geography of the vast region in which they live. The northern part of Central Asia is covered by two of the major deserts of the world, the Gobi and the Taklimakan, which create the only significant geographic barriers within what is otherwise no more than an enormous expanse of plain and taiga. In the deserts people traditionally lived mainly on oases watered by seasonal and sometimes underground rivers. The land there is generally flat, so riverbeds are shallow. At times strong windstorms drive rivers to change their courses completely, causing formerly fertile oases to dry up and forcing the tribespeople who have settled around them to move elsewhere.

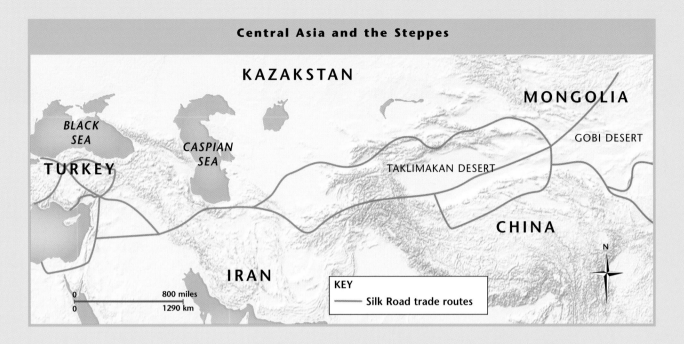

Central Asia and the Steppes

KAZAKSTAN

MONGOLIA

BLACK
SEA

GOBI DESERT

CASPIAN
SEA

TAKLIMAKAN DESERT

TURKEY

CHINA

N

IRAN

| 0 | 800 miles |
| 0 | 1290 km |

KEY
— Silk Road trade routes

Below: In order to leave their native lands, the Mongols had to traverse extremely inhospitable terrain, such as the Outer Mongolian steppes.

With their sources of water constantly changing, people living on the grassy plains developed nomadic cultures, following their herds of sheep and horses to seasonal pastures. The fabled Silk Road, by which goods and ideas were traded between China at one end and Europe and the Middle East at the other, passed straight through the middle of Central Asia, connecting oases across the deserts.

In the early 21st century part of Central Asia and the Steppes is claimed by China as Xinjiang province, while the rest of the region lies within the independent countries of the former Soviet Union. These are Kazakstan, Uzbekistan, Turkmenistan, and Tajikistan in the west, Kyrgyzstan and Mongolia in the north, and, above them, the vast expanse of Siberia, part of modern Russia.

This area was the cradle of two related peoples who had a major impact on world history—the Turks and the Mongols. The Turks began to emerge from Central Asia in the 9th century CE; by the 11th century the Seljuk Turks dominated Persia (Iran). The Mongols came from Mongolia in the 13th century to overrun the Eurasian landmass from the Pacific Ocean almost all the way to the Danube.

In the early 14th century the Ottoman Turks in Anatolia (present-day Turkey) began building an empire that would eventually rule much of southwest Asia and south-central Europe until the end of World War I. As the Mongols and Turks came into increasing contact with other cultures, they were exposed to new religions. Many adopted Islam, although others were converted to Buddhism, Christianity, and Manichaeanism.

The Turks and Mongols began using writing after they came into contact with other cultures. The most ancient

Left: This illustration is from a 16th-century edition of the book The Secret History of the Mongols; *it depicts Genghis Khan and his Mongol army conquering the Khitan and Jurje tribes.*

Shamanism

Originally the Turks and Mongols practiced various forms of shamanism, which has been described as the earliest type of religion to emerge in human society. It is a highly decentralized religious system, in which theology and organized priesthood play little or no part. Shamans were thought to possess the ability to induce a trance in which the soul left the body and traveled to the "otherworld" inhabited by spirits and gods. There the shaman negotiated with the deities for the benefit of the tribe. Shamanic cultures think of the universe as consisting of at least three layers: the upper world, the underworld, and the middle, human world. These are usually connected by an exceptionally high mountain or a World Tree, which passes through the center point of the universe and is often referred to as the Axis Mundi (the axis of the world) or the omphalos (focal point).

The traditional roles of the shaman were to make deals with the Master or Mistress of Animals for a successful hunt, to retrieve the souls of ailing members of the tribe whose sickness had been diagnosed as "soul loss," or to guide the newly dead soul to the next world. Turkic and Mongol shamans, by the time that written sources offer information on them, were very much involved with reading omens and fortunes, performing sacrifices and purification rituals, and controlling the rain through the use of bezoars. (A bezoar is a hard mass of vegetable fiber or hair that accumulates in the intestines of some grazing animals and is often believed to have magical properties.) The costumes the shamans wore clearly showed their role as mediators between the human and animal spirit worlds by making them appear part human and part animal. Their ceremonial apparel included antlers, feathers, or wings, and was made of fur, adorned with teeth, bones, and even the paws of animals. It may also have had mirrorlike metal plates to reflect the otherworld.

The shaman's ability to go into a trance seems to have been at least in part an innate talent, perhaps the result of certain biases in brain function that set the shaman apart from other people. Some early European ethnographers labeled all shamans as schizophrenic, although that diagnosis is now rejected. The trance could also be induced by drumming, dancing, or chanting, and because of this, musical and poetic inspiration could develop an association between the shaman and the otherworld. In some cultures shamans were restricted to a single sex, most often male,

written sources, therefore, were composed from Islamic or Buddhist perspectives, often by travelers who returned home and described what they had seen. Major sources of information include the 13th-century *Secret History of the Mongols*, which focused on the life of the first great Mongol ruler Genghis Khan (c. 1162–1227) and his sons and grandsons, and the *Oghuznama*, which related the exploits of the ancestor-hero of the Oghuz Turks. External sources range from the writings of early European explorers to Central Asia and the Steppes, such as Marco Polo (1254–1324), to numerous historical texts in which Chinese authors commented on the practices of their invasive neighbors from the north and west.

A Myth of the Origin of Mongol Shamanism

Once upon a time, when the Mongols still lived in their ancestral land of Khangia, there was an old man who knew magic. When he foresaw that his death was approaching, he told his son that if he was buried properly and given offerings, he would continue to protect his family from beyond the grave. As predicted, the father soon died. The son buried him at a high place called Red Rock and made offerings of tea, water, milk, and alcohol on the first, seventh, and ninth day of each full moon. The father's spirit, meanwhile, became friendly with the local spirits of the earth and was able to cause hail, lightning, and bad fortune. When the son's mother died, he buried her in a high place and made sacrifices to her as well. Her spirit became capable of flying, of causing hail, rain, thunder, and lightning, and of poisoning men and livestock. The people discussed how to appease these two powerful spirits, so they joined the son in making offerings and asked the spirits to be merciful. The spirit of the father entered the body of a man and the spirit of the mother entered the body of a woman, both of whom began to tremble uncontrollably. Thereafter, the father's spirit was worshiped as Qara Sakighulsun (Black Protective Spirit) and the mother's was worshiped as Emegelji Eji (Very Old Grandmother).

The man and the woman were able to fly when possessed by the spirits, and one day they flew to the graves of the father and mother, where they found drums and yellow-feathered headpieces. They took these back with them and began singing and drumming. The people offered them tea, milk, water, and alcohol so that the two would protect them from evil. They called them *böge* (male shaman) and *nidughan* (female shaman).

Right: This is an illustration of a nidughan, *a female shaman from Mongolia.*

although Korean shamans, for instance, were female. By contrast, other cultures, such as the Lapps of Finland, made no such distinction between men and women. Likewise, the Turks and Mongols appear to have had both male and female shamans, since there are separate words for the two: *böge* for the male and *nidughan* for the female.

Principal deities

The chief god of the Turks and Mongols was Tengri, a sky god. Scholars believe that he was first mentioned around the second century BCE. Tengri was supported by a mother goddess called Umay, whose name means "placenta" in Turkic. He was also aided by celestial objects such as the sun, the moon, the Pleiades star formation, and the planet Venus. Tengri was sometimes depicted as a single deity, often called Köke Möngke Tengri (Eternal Blue Heaven), but he was also conceived as consisting of either 33 or 99 different *tengris*, who were personifications of abstract concepts such as desire, time, and the road. Roads were particularly important in nomadic cultures. There were also spirits for nearly every object, including specific lands and bodies of water, trees, the cosmic pole that connected the worlds, the threshold, and even the doorjamb.

The fire deity, whose name varied over time but who was most commonly known as Odqan Ghalaqan (Youngest-born Fire-king) or Odqan Ghalaqan Eke

Some Turkic and Mongol Gods

Ai:	Goddess of the moon.
Cholban/Chulpan:	Venus, the morning star.
Dolughan Ebügan:	The constellation Ursa Major.
Erlik:	God of war and underworld.
Koyash:	God of the sun.
Odqan Ghalaqan:	God of fire.
Öd Tengri:	God of time.
Tengri:	Supreme god and a deity of the sky.
Timer Kazyk:	The Pole Star.
Umay:	Goddess of fertility.
Ürker:	The Pleiades.
Yer-Sub:	Goddess of the land, water, and the middle world.
Yol Tengri:	God of the road and luck.
Personified elements:	Water, air, thunder and lightning, wind, tornadoes, clouds, rain, and rainbows.

(Mother Youngest-born Fire-queen), was also very important. The deity's gender varied, although the earliest form appears to have been feminine. The main fire ritual took place at the end of the year, when hymns were recited and the breastbone of a sheep was offered to the deity. Among some Mongol peoples these rituals were performed only by women. Minor rituals took place at seasonal festivals and at weddings, where people asked for blessings and protection. Odqan Ghalaqan was primarily a guardian of the family and its fortune.

As might be expected among nomadic peoples, there were several deities who were associated with horses. These included Sülde, who was a protective spirit embodied by a standard made of horse tails; Dayisun or Dayisud Tengri, who was a mounted war god; and Geser Khan, a protector of warriors and of (horse) herds.

Demons also abounded in Turkic and Mongol religion. Some were the opponents of the shamans, adversaries to be overcome in the struggle to reach the otherworld and negotiate with the gods. Many were the spirits of the unhappy dead, who roamed the earth in search of humans to eat or to lead astray. One type of spirit of the unhappy

Above: These modern Mongols from the Kazak group of the Olgii province play a traditional New Year's game called Bozkashi. The game is performed on horseback and helps the participants to improve their horse-riding skills.

The Oghuzes, Uighurs, and the Huns

The Oghuzes are a Mongol group who traditionally inhabited parts of modern Uzbekistan. The Uighurs are Mongols of northwestern China and adjacent parts of the former Soviet Union. Despite their modern geographical separation, they share a common creation myth. This may indicate that they were once a single group, or that they formerly cohabited much more closely than today. The story in outline is as follows:

Long ago, there was a Hun chieftain who had twin daughters, more beautiful than any women on earth. He decided to keep his daughters locked away from all men, so he built for them a mansion in the highest region of the north of his domain. However, a god came to the two girls in the shape of a blue wolf and married them both. One girl gave birth to the first nine Oghuzes and the other gave birth to the first 10 Uighurs. They became the ancestors of these two groups.

The Huns were a Mongol group who spread southward across the steppes, terrorizing northern China and eastern Europe. Their graves are common in Central Asia and the Steppes. Their best-known monuments are stones with carvings that depict deer with the sun in their antlers. These memorials were probably used in shamanic rituals.

dead was a *yek*, which appeared as a whirlwind of dust; another was a *hortlak*, which dug up corpses in the night to feed on their dead flesh. In the deserts there were believed to be spirits who called to travelers from the sands, luring them off their track to death by dehydration. A demon called Al-Basti (Red Mother) or Al-Karisi (Red Woman) preyed on women during childbirth. She also rode horses in the night and abandoned them, covered in sweat, at dawn, much like the *mara* of European nightmare lore.

Creation myths—a low priority

The Turks and Mongols do not appear to have had a strong myth accounting for the origin of the world or of humans. Their cosmos began with the sky and the earth, between which humans were made by some unspecified act. Likewise, the end of the world was not of great concern. The few surviving references to an apocalypse suggest a belief that eventually the sky would collapse onto the earth, and the middle world would fall into ruin. Generally, the mythology was much more concerned with the origin of specific groups. For instance, the founder of the group was especially revered, and sacrifices were offered at his tomb. In nomadic cultures this was often the one fixed spot in nomadic life.

Animals often featured as totems—representations of ancestors who had taken human form to create the group. In many cultures around the world, including those of the Turks and Mongols, the totemic animal would often be the appropriate sacrifice to the deified ancestor. The most important animals for this purpose were the wolf (often interchangeable with the dog), lion, stag, bear, horse, camel, and serpent or dragon. Birds were also important, especially the eagle (depicted with one or two heads), falcon, swan or goose, crane, and hen and rooster. Except for the camel, an

animal found only in the desert, the symbolism and relative importance of these animals and birds were very similar to their positions in the hierarchies of northern European mythologies such as the Celtic and Germanic.

The most common Central Asian myth of origin concerned a human who was either the child of, or brought up by, a she-wolf. The latter version is similar to the story of the founding of Rome, in which the twins Romulus and Remus were suckled by a wolf. In the earliest form of the Central Asian myth, an abandoned baby boy was nursed by a she-wolf. Later, the myth was changed to the story of a princess who married a wolf and gave birth to a boy. In other versions the child was the sole survivor of a war. He was cast into the marshes by his enemies, where he was discovered and raised by a she-wolf, with whom he later mated. The child was, in other cases, the offspring of a wolf and a deer (the ancestor of Genghis Khan, according to *The Secret History of the Mongols*), a horse and a cow (the Khitan group), a camel and a lion (the Qarakjanids), or a jackal and a woman (the Qalatch).

The ancestor most widely worshiped by the Mongols was their most powerful and important historical leader, Genghis Khan. Like many legendary heroes, such as King Arthur of Britain, he began to acquire the attributes of deities. He was credited with having initiated many important customs, the most important of which were the four seasonal festivals. These were held on the 21st day of the last month of spring (the Feast of the White Herd), the 15th day of the middle month of summer (the Feast of Midsummer), the 12th day of the last month of autumn (the Feast of Autumn Dryness), and the third day of the first month of winter (Memorial Day of the Anointing of the Newborn Genghis). The Mongolian wedding ritual also invoked the name of Genghis Khan, as did blessings on

Above: Much like falconry, Mongolian eagle hunting, as practiced in the western part of Central Asia, is performed with a bird specially trained to kill prey and return to its trainer. In Mongol mythology the eagle was one of the most prominent totemic animals.

hunting equipment and the custom of braiding silk strips into the manes of race-winning horses. Genghis Khan is also recalled in many place-names throughout the region.

Above: Throughout Central Asia and the Steppes, the nomadic Mongols erected shrines, as seen here, made out of stones, wood, and fabric dedicated to their deities. Passersby would add to the shrine.

Life after death

The Turks and Mongols believed in an afterlife that was virtually identical to life on earth, but that took place in the sky. The soul was believed to leave the body, often in the form of a fly or a pigeon, and migrate to the heavens, the abode of the supreme god Tengri. Although there does not appear to have been a belief in a judgment that took place after death, with the good souls going to a heaven and the bad souls going to a hell, it was possible for a soul to get lost on its way to the sky. This was where the shaman became necessary as a guide. There were also rituals, which varied greatly from place to place, that had to be carried out exactly according to custom in order for the soul to complete its journey safely. The soul was believed to be contained in the blood, so it was important not to spill any when the soul was intended to go to the spirit world. Although bloodletting was an acceptable part of animal sacrifices, princes who were ritually sacrificed had to be strangled so that none of their blood was spilled.

As the Turks and Mongols adopted Buddhism and Islam, their shamanism became a folk religion, with laypersons performing rituals such as fire prayers and offerings of incense. The names of deities became amalgamated with those of the new creeds. For example, the chief *tengri* was called Köke Möngke Tengri. However, he was also called Qormusta, which is an adoption of the Iranian deity Ahura Mazda. Qormusta was regarded as equivalent to the Hindu god Brahma, who was called Esrua by the Mongols. With the adoption of Islam, Tengri acquired some of the attributes of Allah. However, in the 20th century, the Communist governments of China and the Soviet Union attempted to stamp out all forms of religious practice. As a reaction against this repression, many people became more observant than they might otherwise have been. The dominant faith in Central Asia and the Steppes became Islam, and this contributed to the decline of shamanism, which Muslims regarded as a redundant superstition.

LESLIE ELLEN JONES

Bibliography

Odigan, Sarangerel, and Julie Ann Stewart. *Riding Windhorses: A Journey into the Heart of Mongolian Shamanism.* Rochester, VT: Destiny Books, 2000.

Roe Metternich, Hilary, ed. *Mongolian Folktales.* Boulder, CO: Avery Press, 1996.

Sermier, Claire, and Helen Loveday, trans. *Mongolia: Empire of the Steppes.* Union Lake, MI: Odyssey Publications, 2002.

SEE ALSO: Ancestor Worship; Blood; Death and the Afterlife; Devils; Festivals; Nature Religions; Shamans.

CHINA

The vast country of China includes people from many different ethnic groups and cultures. Over the centuries many of these people amalgamated their mythologies, so what is thought of as Chinese mythology is actually a blend of philosophies and belief systems.

China as a nation is over four thousand years old, but no written evidence exists from its beginnings, and most theories about the mythological beliefs of the earliest peoples of China are based on archaeological investigation. There is nothing to suggest the existence of an organized and organic mythology in the manner of ancient Greece or ancient Egypt. The earliest written evidence dates from the first Han dynasty (206 BCE–8 CE), but this was a long time after the beginnings of Chinese culture, and modern scholars are uncertain of the extent to which writers of the period modified, invented, or falsified information in their texts. Moreover, many thousands of books were lost in the "burning of the books" in 213 BCE, when Emperor Shih Huang Ti decreed that all written material of a nonpractical nature be destroyed.

The geography and political history of China have had a significant influence on its mythology. Modern China covers a vast area that in ancient times was occupied by numerous distinct ethnic and cultural groups, with many other nomadic peoples living nearby. Over the centuries there was much cross-fertilization between the mythologies and religious beliefs of these groups, even though they were often at war with each other.

Early myths and practices

The oldest graves that have been discovered in China date from around the fourth millennium BCE. In them, archaeologists have found evidence of human sacrifice and "accompanying-in-death," the ritual in which servants and wives were buried with the corpse of a rich or powerful man. Such careful attention to burial practices

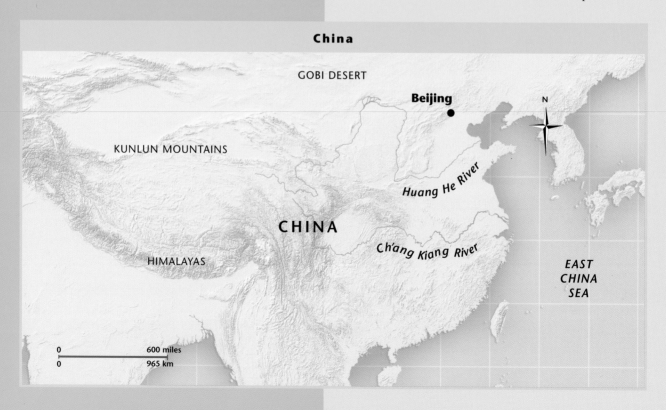

China

GOBI DESERT

Beijing

N

KUNLUN MOUNTAINS

Huang He River

CHINA

Ch'ang Kiang River

HIMALAYAS

EAST CHINA SEA

0 ___ 600 miles
0 ___ 965 km

Above: This photograph shows artifacts buried with bodies in a Neolithic site near Xi'an. The objects were intended to help the dead in the afterlife.

and procedures suggests that ancestor worship was already a strong element of Chinese culture. Reverence for ancestors may also have contributed to the later practice of euhemerism, in which outstanding historical characters were deified after their death. The cult of ancestors appears also to be closely related to the early forms of Chinese worship, in which only the king—as father of the nation—was allowed to worship and offer sacrifices to Shang-Ti ("Supreme Ruler"). People of lower social standing worshiped lesser gods and powers.

Some graves of this period contain evidence of scapulimancy, a form of divination that appears to be unique to China. Scapulimancy involved heating the shoulder blades (Latin: *scapulae*) of mammals with coals or a hot poker and interpreting the cracks thus produced. The practice persisted until the 18th century BCE, during the Shang dynasty. Typical questions asked of oracle bones concerned hunting, fishing, the prospects for the harvest, weather forecasting, sickness, and the correct way to perform sacrifices.

Creation myths

The earliest archaeological evidence for mythological beliefs in China is much more recent, dating from about the fifth century BCE. It suggests that the Chinese were generally more concerned with the structure of the universe than with inventing legends about the manner of its creation.

Such stories do exist, however. According to one, chaos reigned until the emergence from it of yin and yang (see box, page 304), the twin categories of all life and form. These in turn gave shape to heaven and earth respectively, and then to everything else in the universe.

The most popular Chinese creation myth, that of the genial giant Panku, dates from the third century CE. Long before the creation of heaven and earth, chaos had the shape of an egg. Inside this egg Panku was born. After 18,000 years, the egg opened up. The heavier and darker parts, the yin, formed the earth, while the lighter and purer parts, the yang, formed heaven. Every day, Panku grew by 10 feet (3 m), making heaven ascend and the earth thicken by that distance, separating the two elements. After 18,000 years Panku had grown as tall as the distance between heaven and earth.

Right: This illustration shows Ch'ang O drinking a stolen elixir of life before fleeing to the moon, where she became queen.

Later versions of the story make Panku the origin of all the features of the universe. When he died, his head became the four cardinal mountains, his eyes the sun and the moon, his body fat the rivers and seas, his hair the plants. A later embellishment claims that man was created from the fleas on Panku's body.

The story of Panku later became linked to Taoist traditions. Taoism is a Chinese philosophical belief system based on *Tao-te Ching* and other writings credited to the philosopher Lao-tzu (c. 604–531 BCE), but probably written more than 300 years earlier. It advocates a simple, honest life and noninterference with the course of natural events. *Tao* means "path" or "flow"; those who follow the Tao cease to strive, and live in effortless harmony with the principles of the universe.

As Taoism developed, it acquired religious aspects, incorporating earlier strands of Chinese belief, and established monastic orders and lay masters, as well as its own gods and goddesses.

The structure of the world

The oldest known Chinese account of the structure of the world held that heaven was shaped like an upturned bowl covering Earth. It revolved on its own axis, the Pole Star, which was the highest point of heaven. The stars were fixed on its inner surface and turned with it. Earth was a flat, square surface, surrounded by oceans on its four sides. Heaven was supported by pillars (the number varies, depending on the source), which were often identified with mountains, while Earth was supported by eight columns. Heaven had nine levels, the Nine Heavens, each one of which had a gate guarded by tigers and panthers. Below Earth were the Yellow Springs, which were sometimes held to be the realm of the dead. There were 10 suns, appearing one after the other in the sky. They traveled in a chariot drawn by six dragon-horses from the Shining Valley in the east to the tree *po* in the west. Nine of the suns remained in the lower branches of the tree while one of them climbed to the top and threw itself into the sky.

One related legend tells how, during a period of great disorder, all 10 suns appeared together in the sky. The heat was so intense that it threatened to destroy all life on Earth, but at the last moment Hou-I, the Lord Archer, equipped with a magical bow given to him by a mythical emperor, shot down nine of the suns. The myth explains why there is now only one sun.

Yin and Yang

The twin principles of yin and yang are fundamental to the Chinese view of the structure and working of everything in the universe. Present since they came together out of primordial chaos, yin and yang are opposite but complementary principles. All phenomena, all aspects of life, consist of the two principles in differing degrees. Yang is male, heaven, light, dry, and active. Yin is the opposite: female, earth, dark, wet, and passive. The interaction between the two principles determines the way the universe and all that is in it work. In the traditional art of East Asia, the harmony of the two elements is frequently symbolized by a circle divided by an S-shaped curve into two halves of contrasting colors, as in the national flag of South Korea.

The Chinese naturalist school of philosophy, which is thought to have been established by Zou Yan in the fourth century BCE, adopted a closely related set of categories called the five elements (or phases)—wood, earth, fire, metal, and water. By the first Han dynasty (206 BCE– 8 CE), the yin-yang concept had been adopted by nearly all other schools of Chinese philosophy and incorporated into a system of divination that was authorized and sponsored by the state.

Left: Above a sacred lion hang the interlocking symbols of yin and yang, the two complementary principles of cosmic energy.

According to this system of belief, there were also 12 moons, following each other in the sky month by month. At the beginning of each month the Mother of the Moons washed her children in a lake at the western edge of the world. The moon then made its journey through the sky, drawn, like the sun, in a chariot.

Hou-I's wife was Ch'ang O, the moon goddess. When he found that she had stolen his potion of immortality, she took refuge in the moon. Ch'ang O's legendary beauty is celebrated in many works of art and literature. Sometimes she is shown accompanied by a hare while preparing the potion of immortality. More often she is seen holding a moon disk in her right hand.

The mythical emperors of the Golden Age

Myths dating back to the early Chou dynasty (12th to 7th centuries BCE) tell of a golden age of 10 mythical emperors, the inventors of techniques and creators of works beneficial to mankind. The first of these mythical emperors was Fu Hsi, also known as T'ai Hao (the Great Shining One), born in the 29th century BCE as a divine being with a serpent's head. Fu Hsi domesticated animals and

The I Ching

The I Ching (Book of Changes) is an ancient text whose origins date from more than three thousand years ago. It is used for divination and guidance in all matters. It consists mainly of 64 symbolic hexagrams (six-pointed star-shaped figures), which, if interpreted correctly, are said to help understand or even influence events. The hexagrams are formed by joining in pairs the eight basic trigrams (triangular figures), which, according to tradition, were discovered by the legendary emperor Fu Hsi in the 29th century BCE. The trigrams are accompanied by texts, interpretations, and seven philosophical commentaries. Some scholars believe that the commentaries may have been the work of the philosopher Confucius.

The I Ching is one of the Five Classics, the defining works of Confucianism. The other four are Shu Ching (Book of History), Shih Ching (Book of Odes), Li Chi (Book of Rites), and Ch'un Ch'iu (Spring and Autumn Annals). These writings set out the philosopher's ethical system, which emphasizes moral order, the humanity and virtue of China's ancient rulers, and gentlemanly education. Since the second century BCE, the Five Classics have carried as much moral authority in China as the Judeo-Christian Bible has had in the West.

Right: A silk purse and three magical coins were used for consulting the I Ching.

taught people how to cook, fish with nets, and hunt with iron weapons. A later tradition credits him with the invention of the trigrams, used for divination, of the I Ching (see box, above).

The second mythical emperor in this tradition was Shen Nong (the Divine Husbandman), who had the head of a bull and the body of a man. He established agriculture, inventing the cart and the plow, and taught the people how to clear the land with fire. He was said to have been able to speak at the age of three days, to walk at a week, and to plow a field by the time he was three.

Shen Nong's long reign was followed by the brief one of Yen Ti, who was overthrown by his brother, the great Huang Ti, the Yellow Emperor. Huang Ti introduced wooden houses, boats, and carts; he cleared the forests for cattle breeding, established many government institutions, and coined the first money. He was also credited with the invention of writing. Huang Ti was a great warrior, defeating "barbarians" in a great battle and uniting the tribes of the Yellow River (Huang He) plain. His reign exemplified the Golden Age, during which the emperor ruled for the benefit of all in accordance with the natural law. A later Taoist myth held that, on his death, Huang Ti was carried off to heaven on the back of a dragon and became an immortal. The Yellow Emperor has remained a popular figure in China through to the modern era.

Of the next three legendary emperors—Shao Hao, Chen Hsu, and K'u—relatively little is recorded, but the emperor who follows them, Yao, is the model of the wise ruler, acting always in accordance with the harmony of the universe. He was later singled out for particular praise by Confucius (551–479 BCE), the great philosopher whose posthumously collected thoughts, the *Analects*, became the official Chinese creed from the second century BCE. Yao's reign was a period of peace, plenty, stability, and social harmony, and his great wisdom was shown when he passed over his own son for the succession in favor of a virtuous

Left: This ornately carved red lacquer box from the 18th century CE is decorated with the image of a dragon.

peasant, Shun. Yao tested Shun in various ways before abdicating in his favor. Yao then served as counselor to the new emperor, who is credited with standardizing weights and measures and with dividing China into provinces.

Yao's reign was blighted by a series of great floods, which continued under Shun. Yao chose Kun—one of the eight sons of Chen Hsu and father of the future emperor Ta Yü—to combat the deluges. Kun attempted to dam the waters, perhaps by stealing from heaven some magic soil. This was held to be a violation of the natural order, and the floods continued. Shun imprisoned Kun until his death. Three years later Kun's preserved body was cut open and his son, Ta Yü (Yü the Great), came forth.

Ta Yü, known as the Tamer of the Flood, was one of China's great heroes. Rather than damming the waters, he dug channels, pierced tunnels, and "led the rivers to the sea," laboring for 10 years until he became lame in one leg.

These myths reflect a perennial Chinese preoccupation—much of the nation's most heavily populated and agriculturally productive areas lie in the basins of great rivers, the longest of which, the Ch'ang Kiang (Yangtze Kiang), flows 3,965 miles (6,380 km) and drains a basin of 700,000 square miles (1.8 million sq km). In its lower reaches it converges with the Huang He (Yellow River), which extends for 2,900 miles (4,670 km) and is sometimes known as "China's sorrow." China's rivers often flood, with potentially disastrous results, and their water level has always been one of the key determiners of the nation's prosperity.

Ta Yü is considered the founder of the unverified Hsia dynasty (22nd to 18th centuries BCE), which immediately preceded the Shang, the earliest dynasty of which there is historical evidence.

Mountains

Mountains have been important in China since the most ancient times, as both the recipients and locations of sacrifice. Mountains are near to heaven, the rain-bearing clouds form around them, and they are thought of as worlds in themselves, full of virtuous properties and creatures.

There are many local sacred mountains, but on a global scale there are four cardinal mountains, placed at the four corners of the earth, with some traditions placing a fifth at the center. The most prominent is Tai Shan, the cardinal mountain of the west. This is thought to have been a place of pilgrimage and sacrifice since the third millennium BCE, and legend has it that 72 emperors have made the pilgrimage there. Popular tradition says that after death souls return to a kind of underworld found at the foot of Tai Shan.

Besides the cardinal mountains there are many mythical mountains. The most famous of these is Kunlun, at the extreme west of the known world. High enough to touch heaven, Kunlun is connected to several myths concerning immortality. It is the place where the Queen Mother of the West lives and grows the sacred peaches of immortality.

Below: A rainbow in cloudy skies arcs over the sacred mountains of the eastern Kunlun Range in the A'nyêmagên Range, China.

The Taoist pantheon

In the latter centuries of the Chou dynasty (sometime between the seventh and third centuries BCE), a new mythology began to take shape in China. In many respects this school of thought mirrored China's earthly organization, reflecting an increased centralization of power and a highly structured administration. Some of the divinities in this mythology seem to be derived from Buddhism, which reached China in the first century CE. Most, however, are of Taoist origin, some deriving from a learned and aristocratic strain, others from the popular and agrarian tradition. Many of these divinities achieved later popularity through their portrayal in two novels of the Ming dynasty (15th century CE), *Travels in the West* and *Romance of the Investiture of the Gods*.

At the top of the divine Taoist hierarchy reigned the Jade Emperor (Yü Ti), also known as the Jade August Supreme Lord (Yü Huang Shang Ti). The latter name was conferred on him when he was officially sanctioned as a deity by the emperors of the Sung dynasty (960–1279 CE).

Chinese Deities

Ch'ang O:	Moon goddess.
Chen Hsu:	Sixth of the 10 mythical emperors of the Golden Age.
Ch'eng Huang:	Deity that guards cities and towns.
Fu Hsi:	First emperor of the Golden Age.
Fu Hsing:	A god of the Fu–Shou–Lu trinity.
Fu Shen:	A god of the Fu–Shou–Lu trinity.
Hou-I:	The Lord Archer.
Huang Ti:	Fourth mythical emperor of the Golden Age.
K'u:	Seventh mythical emperor of the Golden Age.
K'uei Hsing:	Dwarf god of examinations.
Panku:	Originator of the universe.
Shang-Ti:	The Supreme Ruler.
Shao Hao:	Fifth of the 10 mythical emperors of the Golden Age.
Shen Nong:	Second of the 10 mythical emperors.
Shou-Hsing:	God of longevity.
Shun:	Ninth mythical emperor of the Golden Age.
Ta Yü:	Last emperor of Golden Age; the Tamer of the Flood.
Ts'ai Shen:	Taoist god of wealth.
Tsao Shen:	Domestic hearth god.
T'u-ti:	Any of the gods of small places.
Yao:	Eighth mythical emperor of the Golden Age.
Yü Ti:	The Jade Emperor, supreme Taoist deity.
Wang Mu:	The Queen Mother of the West, wife of Yü Ti.
Wen Ti:	God of literature.

Right: This ivory figurine of Shou-Hsing was carved between about 1550 and 1640 CE.

He is usually shown sitting on a throne, wearing the imperial robes and cap and holding a special jade ceremonial tablet.

The Jade Emperor resided in a heavenly court, where he was surrounded by subordinate deities who mirrored the functions of the earthly court and bureaucracy. His wife was the Queen Mother Wang (Wang Mu), a popular version of the more ancient Queen Mother of the West (Hsi Wang Mu). Like her predecessor, Wang Mu presided over the banquets of the immortals at which many delicacies, including the peach of immortality, were served. She is usually represented as a young woman in ceremonial dress with attendant peacocks or ladies-in-waiting.

Gods of learning

Literature and examinations have always been very important in Chinese culture, and there were Taoist gods of both activities. The main responsibilities of the god of literature, Wen Ti (or Wen Ch'ang), were to watch over writers and to reward or punish them as they deserved. The Jade Emperor appointed him to this job only after the god had lived through 17 reincarnations. In art, Wen Ti is usually represented sitting, wearing a mandarin robe, and carrying a scepter.

K'uei Hsing, Wen Ti's principal assistant, was the god of examinations. He was an ugly but brilliant dwarf, usually represented in the act of running while standing on top of a turtle. In one hand he carried a seal (or a basket), and in the other a brush with which he ticked off the names of the examination candidates on a paper belonging to the Jade Emperor. Originally a mortal named Chung K'uei, K'uei Hsing passed his examinations with great distinction but was refused the usual honors by the emperor, who

Right: This illustration depicts Wen Ti (or Wen Ch'ang), the Chinese god of literature, surrounded by scribes and other helpers.

could not bear to look on his ugliness. K'uei Hsing tried to drown himself, but was carried off to safety on the back of a turtle, a traditional symbol of immortality in China.

Gods of happiness

Three gods, collectively known as Fu-Shou-Lu, watched over the well-being of mankind. The most important was the god of longevity, Shou-Hsing, sometimes also known as "the old man of the South Pole." He is usually depicted with a white beard and a large bald head, leaning on a stick and holding the peach of immortality. He is often with a turtle or a stork, another symbol of long life.

The second of these gods was Fu Hsing, one of many deities who granted happiness to his worshipers—assuming, of course, that they deserved it. He was sometimes identified with the third of the triad, Fu Shen, a deified mandarin of the sixth century BCE. Fu Shen interceded with the emperor on behalf of dwarfs, who were being taken from their families to work as court servants and entertainers. His appeal was successful, and the dwarfs thereafter established a cult to their benefactor.

Guardian deities of place

Every city and large town had its Ch'eng Huang (in Chinese, "wall and moat"), a guardian deity appointed by the Jade Emperor. There is no mention of Ch'eng Huang before the sixth century CE, and it is believed that the origin of a Ch'eng Huang was often a local official, deified for his good service to the community. Officials might go to the Ch'eng Huang with a difficult problem, hoping that the answer would be revealed to them in a dream. Once or twice a year an effigy of the god would be carried through the streets to inspect the city, while relatives would visit the Ch'eng Huang to report a death or a birth so that community records could be kept up to date. Each smaller town and village, as well as every bridge, house, and field, also had its own god of place, the T'u-ti. They were usually deified historical people.

Every individual home had its hearth god, or Tsao Shen. Once a year he would report to the Jade Emperor, who allotted the family the happiness it deserved. Before the hearth god's departure from his traditional place above the kitchen stove, sweet food was smeared over the lips of his paper image, which was then ceremonially burned. At the start of each new year a fresh paper image would be put up to welcome him on his return from the emperor. Homes

also had door gods, called Men Shen. They were warlike figures whose images were placed on either side of the front door. Their purpose was to prevent evil spirits from entering the house.

In the Taoist popular pantheon Ts'ai Shen, the god of wealth, heads a large ministry of wealth. He is worshiped particularly during the New Year festivities.

PETER CONNOR

Bibliography

Allan, Sarah. *The Shape of the Turtle: Myth, Art, and Culture in Early China.* New York, NY. State University of New York Press, 1991.

Werner, E.T.C. *Myths and Legends of China.* New York, NY. Dover Publications, 1994

SEE ALSO: Ancestor Worship; Calendars; Deities; Dragons; Korea; Moon; Southeast Asia; Sun.

CIRCE

Circe is best known from Homer's *Odyssey*, in which she plays a leading role in one of Odysseus's most important adventures. She is immortal and inhabits an island somewhere in the distant ocean, where she lives alone except for her magic servants and tame wild animals, lions and wolves that fawn on her like dogs. These are actually men she has magically transformed.

When Odysseus and his men landed on Circe's island, the goddess received them kindly, but the food she served was laced with a drug that made them drowsy. Once it had taken effect, she struck the men with a rod and turned them all into pigs, except for Odysseus. He would have suffered the same fate, too, had the god Hermes not met him previously and given him the moly plant (a species of lily), which protected him from Circe's spells.

Because Odysseus could resist Circe, she recognized him as the hero who she had been told by an earlier prophecy would one day come to her. She turned his men back into human shape, younger and more handsome than before, and became Odysseus's friend and lover.

The men stayed with Circe for a year. She told them that they must visit the land of the dead, and when they went there Odysseus was given a prophecy of his own death. They then returned to Circe for further instructions. She told them to depart, but not before warning them of the dangers of the journey ahead. In particular, she told them not to kill the cattle of the sun god, Helios, which lived on the island of Thrinacia. As it turned out, only Odysseus was resolute enough to heed her warning, and consequently he was the only member of the crew to complete the journey.

Circe also features in the story of Jason and the Argonauts. According to Apollonius of Rhodes, when the *Argo* came to Circe's island, the goddess anointed Jason and Medea with pig's blood so that they could atone for their theft of the Golden Fleece. Medea and Circe were close relatives—they were both descended from Helios. The daughters and granddaughters of Helios were dangerous women; another was Pasiphae, mother of the Minotaur.

In a later version of the Circe myth, Odysseus left the goddess pregnant. When their son, Telegonus, grew up, he went in search of his father. He came by chance to Ithaca, and, not knowing where he was, raided the island. Odysseus rushed to fight him off. Telegonus, unaware that this threatening figure was his own father, killed him. This fulfilled the prophecy made to Odysseus in the underworld that his death would come from the sea. Telegonus then

Right: Circe has captured the imagination of artists throughout the ages. This bronze figurine on a marble pedestal is the work of the Australian sculptor Edgar Bertram Mackennal (1863–1931).

Left: This 1580 oil painting by Alessandro Allori (1535–1607) depicts Circe with the companions of Ulysses, whom she has turned into animals.

married Penelope; he and his half-brother Telemachus took Penelope with them back to Circe's island, where Telemachus married Circe. Circe then made the three of them immortal.

Comparable figures

Some scholars have seen in Circe a version of the forest witch familiar from Indo-European folktales such as the story of Hansel and Gretel. Others have suggested that Circe shares characteristics with the West Asian "Mistress of Animals," who has various names, including Ishtar, Lillith, and Anat. The name Circe means "hawk" in Greek, and the comparable West Asian goddesses are often depicted with the wings of hawks or associated with other birds of prey. In the *Epic of Gilgamesh* there are further parallels between Circe and Ishtar, the fertility goddess of the Assyrians and Babylonians: Both can control wild animals; their characters have a dangerous side connected to sexuality and magic; and they both ultimately turn from a threat into a helper. Ishtar turns her lovers into wild animals by striking them with a rod. She also sends her husband down into the underworld. These similarities can hardly be coincidental—the myths of the two deities are interdependent, and possibly come from a common source.

Circe seems to stand mythologically for the dangers (from a male point of view) of sexual entanglement. Those who yield to her attractions may find themselves irreversibly transformed. She has links to the world of the dead, as if her attractions could be not only transformative but also lethal. She is powerful, and if her initial threat can be overcome she becomes beneficent. She is a wise woman, and the transformations she effects may be positive. The lovers who can weather the storm of her early hostility are generally enriched by their subsequent involvement with her.

JAMES M. REDFIELD

Bibliography

Bulfinch, Thomas. *Myths of Greece and Rome.* New York, NY: Viking Penguin, Inc., 1998.
Homer, and Robert Fagles, trans. *The Odyssey.* New York: Penguin USA, 1999.

SEE ALSO: Crete; Daedalus; Dionysus; Ishtar; Minos; Pasiphae; Poseidon; Theseus; Zeus.

CLYTEMNESTRA

Clytemnestra is one of the most vilified characters in Greek mythology because of her adultery and murderous deeds. She took a lover while her husband, King Agamemnon of Mycenae, was away fighting at the Trojan War, and then she killed him on his return.

Below: Dating from around 500 BCE, this vase painting depicts Clytemnestra being restrained by one of Agamemnon's aides, Thaltybios.

The story of Clytemnestra (or Klytaimestra) and the murders she committed was presented in several different versions. The earliest depiction of her, by the Greek poet Homer (c. ninth–eighth century BCE), presents her as a malleable character who was led astray by her lover, Aegisthus. However, later depictions of Clytemnestra by dramatists including Aeschylus, Euripides, and Sophocles generally show her as a heartless character who either led or orchestrated the killings.

Clytemnestra was the daughter of Tyndareos, king of Sparta, and Leda. Her sister was Helen (and sometimes Timandra), and her brothers were Castor and Pollux. According to some sources Helen and Pollux were the immortal children of Zeus, while Clytemnestra and the others were the mortal offspring of Tyndareos. Both Zeus and Tyndareos had slept with Leda on the same night, each making her pregnant with a boy and a girl.

According to one version of the Clytemnestra story, Agamemnon was not her first husband. She was originally married to Tantalus, the son of the Greek prince Thyestes, and they had a son. Agamemnon, who was Thyestes' nephew and ruler of Mycenae, killed both Tantalus and the boy, then married Clytemnestra. Clytemnestra and Agamemnon had three daughters and a son who each featured in dramatic stories of their own, all of which involved their mother. The daughters were Iphigeneia, Chrysothemis, and Electra; the son was Orestes. (In the *Iliad* the daughters were named Chrysothemis, Laodike, and Iphianassa).

The murders

The story of Clytemnestra starts when her sister Helen is abducted by Paris, the incident that began the 10-year Trojan War between Greece and Troy. Helen was married to Menelaus, Agamemnon's brother, and when the war began Agamemnon became leader of the Greek forces. In an effort to ensure strong winds for his ships' speedy journey across the sea, Agamemnon sacrificed Iphigeneia. According to Aeschylus's play *Agamemnon*, Clytemnestra never forgave her husband for the death of Iphigeneia. In *Iphigeneia Among the Taurians*, a play by Euripides, at the moment the girl's throat was about to be cut, divine intervention made her vanish and a deer appear in her place on the altar.

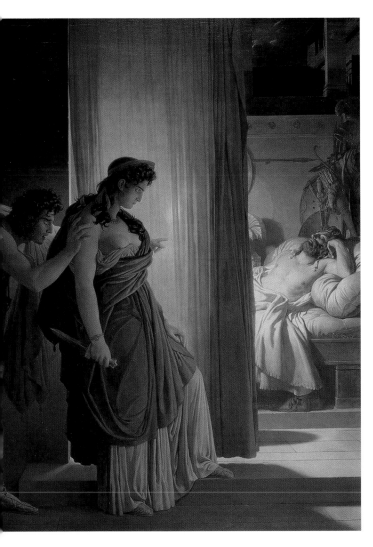

Above: This 1817 painting by French artist Pierre-Narcisse Guérin depicts the moment before Clytemnestra and her lover stab Agamemnon.

While Agamemnon was away fighting in Troy, Clytemnestra began an affair with Aegisthus. When Agamemnon returned victorious to Mycenae, he brought with him his new mistress, Cassandra. Cassandra was the daughter of Priam, the defeated king of Troy. She was clairvoyant but cursed that no one would ever heed her warnings. Soon after their arrival, Clytemnestra stabbed (or axed) Agamemnon and Cassandra to death. When Orestes grew up, he and his sister, Electra, avenged the death of their father by killing both Aegisthus and Clytemnestra.

Dramatists and Clytemnestra

Clytemnestra held particular fascination for Athenian tragedians writing in the fifth and early fourth centuries BCE Aeschylus made Agamemnon's murder and its consequences the focus of his trilogy the *Oresteia*. In the first of the three plays, *Agamemnon*, the king, newly arrived home from the Trojan War, is murdered by his wife and her lover. In the second play, *Choephoroe* (or *The Libation Bearers*), Orestes returns to avenge his father by killing Clytemnestra and Aegisthus. He is guided by the god Apollo and encouraged by Electra, who has waited many years for Orestes' return. The title of the third play, *Eumenides*, is a reference to the Erinyes, or Furies, of Clytemnestra. The Erinyes were spirits that tormented those who wronged relatives, and in Aeschylus's play they drive Orestes insane because he killed his mother. With the help of the goddess Athena, however, Orestes is acquitted of murder at the court of the Areopagus in Athens, and the Erinyes are placated and given a new name, the Eumenides (Kindly Ones).

Although the major Greek dramatists represented Clytemnestra as a faithless wife and unloving mother, each characterized her differently. Aeschylus's Clytemnestra is at first a proud and regal figure, capable of masterful speech and manly deeds. *Choephoroe* depicts her as increasingly fearful of dreams and portents, and terrified when Orestes, whom she thought was long dead, reappears. She dies in the play while begging her son to spare her life.

The Clytemnestra of Sophocles' tragedy *Electra* is more openly hostile to her children, exulting over a false report of Orestes' death and berating Electra for moping about the death of her father. Euripides' *Electra* portrays a vain and hypocritical Clytemnestra, who is lured to her death by Electra's supposedly imminent childbirth. The relationship between the mother and daughter in the play is without love; the two women are deadly rivals.

In the early 20th century, Clytemnestra featured in two important dramatic works, *Elektra* (1909), an opera by the composer Richard Strauss (1864–1949), and *Mourning Becomes Electra* (1931), a trilogy by American playwright Eugene O'Neill (1888–1953). Strauss's opera is based on Sophocles' *Electra*, and O'Neill's trilogy is an adaptation of Aeschylus's *Oresteia*, with the drama being set in post–Civil War New England.

DEBORAH LYONS

Bibliography

Aeschylus, and Robert Fagles, trans. *The Oresteia.* New York: Penguin USA, 1984.

Euripides, and David Grene and Richmond Lattimore, eds. *The Complete Greek Tragedies: Euripides.* Chicago, IL: University of Chicago Press, 1992.

Komar, Kathleen L. *Reclaiming Klytemnestra: Revenge or Reconciliation.* Champaign, IL: University of Illinois Press, 2003.

SEE ALSO: Agamemnon; Atreus; Cassandra; Castor and Pollux; Electra; Furies; Helen; Iphigeneia; Orestes.

CREATION MYTHS

Creation myths helped early cultures give meaning to their lives and their place in the world. Although in general the myths vary from culture to culture, there are some striking similarities between those of ancient civilizations, even those living continents apart.

Humans have always asked how life, earth, and the heavens came to be. Ancient peoples found consoling answers in their imagination and created stories that satisfied both their curiosity and their love of storytelling. Creation myths, also known as cosmogonic myths, tend to deal in opposites, such as darkness and light, sky (heaven) and earth, that at the very beginning are one. Cosmogonic myths also tell of primordial times where the laws of science and nature did not exist and often the world was populated by deities, giants, and other mythic creatures. Yet through the act of creation, the darkness and light are separated, the sky and earth are formed, and in most cases the mythic creatures are vanquished. The world is finally made ready for the creation of humans—specifically the particular culture or group telling the story—who are put at the center of everything.

Creation myths can be categorized generally as being one of, or having the elements of, five different types. In one, the world is created by a single deity who wanted it to be a certain way; his plan may be disrupted, often by a lesser deity. A second type makes the birth of the world similar to the development of a fetus, and often involves a mother goddess who symbolizes earth. In a third version, creation is the product of a union between earth and sky. Other accounts describe a cosmic egg that breaks open to form heaven and earth. The fifth type describes the world as having formed out of land retrieved from primordial waters.

Supreme creators

One of the oldest known creation myths featuring a supreme deity comes from the Zoroastrian belief system, which flourished in Persia (part of modern Iran) some 2,600 years ago. Founded by the religious philosopher Zoroaster, the mythology dismissed all deities of the pantheon that existed in Persia at the time, except for Ahura Mazda, or Ormazd, the supreme creator. Zoroastrianism was a dualist religion, with Ahura Mazda representing light, wisdom, and goodness, and Ahriman—similar to the biblical Satan—controlling darkness and evil. The focus of the mythology is not on how Ahura Mazda, in the form of Ormazd, created the world, but on the battles between Ormazd and Ahriman for control of the world and for the hearts and souls of humankind.

In North America the Pima Indians, who lived in the Southwest, describe how in the beginning only darkness and water existed. Then from a clump of dark matter emerged the Creator, who became conscious and molded a little ball that grew to become the earth. Out of his own flesh the Creator took two bowls of water, from which he made light. The Salish peoples of the North American west coast believed that Amotken was the creator deity. An old benevolent man who dwelled alone in the heavens, Amotken was always watching over his creation.

In Africa the creator deity for the Ibo peoples of Nigeria is Chuku, also called Chineke (Creator). Chuku is believed to be wholly good and only able to create good. According to one myth, he even tried to give humans everlasting life. Chuku sent a messenger dog to his newly created humans to explain that when a person died the others should place the corpse on the ground and cover it with ashes. This would make the dead person live again. The messenger dog, however, grew tired and hungry on his long journey and never made it to the humans. So instead, Chuku sent a sheep with the same message, but when the sheep arrived at the home of the humans, it forgot the exact wording. Mistakenly, the sheep said that the dead were to be buried, and the Ibo had no choice but to do as the sheep instructed, which is why the dead stay dead.

Khonvum, the creator deity for some peoples of central Africa, is in some ways very similar to the Judeo-Christian God in that the deity is believed to have existed before

Right: The Chinese goddess Nü Kua was originally two separate beings, the first man and woman, who were united to form a deity with a woman's head and a snake's body.

creation and would continue to exist for eternity. After creating the earth and the sky, Khonvum lowered from the sky the first humans and gave them the forest filled with fruit and berries to gather and animals to hunt. Unlike the Judeo-Christian God, however, each night Khonvum collects the stars and gives them to the sun so that it can shine the next day.

The Hindu belief system, which originated in India, recognizes many deities, but ruling over them is a single god with three separate identities. The supreme god is Vishnu, and his three identities correspond to the three stages of the cycle of creation. He is known as Brahma when he is creating the earth and humans, Vishnu when he is the guardian of life, and Siva when he destroys all creation before the cycle begins again with Brahma.

Mother goddesses

Early in the development of ancient cultures, societies that were based on agriculture tended to practice a belief system that was centered on an earth mother or female creator deity. This mother goddess not only gave birth to the world, she also nourished it. She symbolized and, it was believed, controlled the agricultural phases throughout the year, from planting to harvesting. In other words, she was the source of all life and order.

In the Japanese pantheon of the Shinto mythology, the goddess Amaterasu is the supreme deity. She is also known as Great Goddess or Mother Goddess. Amaterasu is responsible for fertility, the sun, and the universe, as well as being ruler of the other gods—she did not, however, create humans. Having a female deity as the embodiment of the sun is rare in existing world mythologies, and it is probable that Amaterasu was originally a typical mother goddess from a pre-Shinto culture.

Anthropologists believe that around 2400 BCE the agricultural, matriarchal-based cultures began to be defeated by warrior tribes with patriarchal belief systems. This usurpation of cultures had a lasting effect on the perception of the Mother Goddess and her role in mythologies. From then on supreme female deities were either wedded to warrior gods, superseded by male deities, or transformed into evil goddesses striving to introduce chaos.

In ancient Babylonia Tiamat is an example, some believe, of a mother goddess from an earlier culture who was changed into an evil female dragon that brought chaos.

Left: This ancient statue is of a mother goddess from the Indus Valley (also called Harappan) civilization of the Indian subcontinent. According to archaeologists, the civilization existed from 2500 BCE to 1700 BCE.

In this myth Tiamat threatened to destroy the other gods. Only Marduk, a young male deity, volunteered to do battle with her. He succeeded in killing the goddess dragon, and cut her body into little pieces out of which sky, earth, and people were created. This story comes from the *Enuma Elish*, the ancient Babylonian epic, which may have originated around 1900 BCE. It was written in cuneiform (wedge-shaped) script on seven clay tablets.

In pre-Hindu India the female deity Shakti was the source of all life. She could bestow the gift of energy and fertility and was embodied in rivers such as the Ganges, or Mother Ganga. She later appears as the consort of Vishnu and is variously called Kamala, Padma, or Lakshmi. She rises in the form of a lotus blossom from the navel of Vishnu, who then creates the universe. All elements have their source in these figures, and to them all things return.

Primordial parents

In some cultures the creation myth echoed the human process of reproduction, with a male deity and a female deity copulating to make the world. In Japanese Shinto mythology, for example, the brother-sister couple Izanami (female) and Izanagi (male) were descendants of a small group of first-generation deities. Together they created all the other major

Nut

Nut, a creator deity, was an ancient Egyptian goddess. Scant evidence remains of her cult except hieroglyphic images. She was seen as the daughter of Re, the sun god, and sometimes as his mother. Nut, as the sky goddess, was also believed to have mated with Geb, the earth god, to give birth to Isis, Osiris, and other major deities of the Egyptian pantheon. Scholars believe that Nut was probably the Great Mother before the masculine Re was invented. Later, she was demoted in favor of the sun god. She is usually depicted naked with long arms and legs and standing over the earth in a four-legged posture. Her belly is the sky and has stars attached to it. She wears a vase on her head from which she dispenses the water of life to the dead, while from her breasts milk pours down on earth. She is sometimes conflated with Hathor, the cow goddess, and has a European parallel in the primal Norse cow, Audhumla, and the sacred cow of India. Women, cattle, and sows shared a divine status as fertility symbols from roughly 10,000 to 3000 BCE. After that time, their myths became intermingled with those of the male sky gods and their children.

Below: The top left scene in this Egyptian illustration depicts Geb separating from Nut as described in one version of creation.

deities, including Amaterasu, as well as the earth. However, their primary importance appears to lie in the resolution of their quarrel over death. According to the story, Izanami died while giving birth to fire. She then descended into the underworld. Izanagi went after his sister-wife but was halted by Izanami at the cavernous entrance to the realm of the dead. He pleaded with her to return to the land of the living. She said that she would have to consult the gods of death, and that he was not to enter the underworld while she was away. Izanami was gone a long time, and Izanagi grew impatient. He walked into the dark cave and saw maggots everywhere and the corpse of Izanami decomposing on the ground. Disgusted by what he saw, Izanagi fled the cave pursued by an army of rotting warriors.
At the entrance

Izanagi turned around to see Izanami chasing him too. To stop the demon warriors, Izanagi rolled a huge bolder over the entrance to the cave to prevent them from getting out. Izanami was angry and said that she would take the lives of a thousand people each day from the land of the living because Izanagi had entered the underworld against her wishes. In response, Izanagi said that each day he would make sure that 1,500 women gave birth.

The Greek primordial couple

Another primordial couple were the ancient Greek Uranus (sky) and Gaia (earth). Gaia gave birth to Uranus and then the pair mated, in turn giving birth to the second generation of primordial deities: the Titans, the hundred-handed giants called the Hecatoncheires, and the one-eyed giants known as the Cyclopes. Uranus grew jealous of his mighty children and forced them back into Gaia's body. In pain the Mother Goddess called on her offspring for help, and Cronus, the youngest Titan, volunteered. With Gaia's help, Cronus castrated Uranus, and from his blood falling into the ocean was created the first Olympian deity, the goddess Aphrodite.

In another story it was Prometheus, one of the Titans, who gave the first men the use of fire. Angered by this, Zeus made the god Hephaestus create the first woman, Pandora, who unleashed all the ills and troubles of humankind.

Another common example of primordial couples and creation involved the separation of the pair to distinguish the earth, usually the female deity, from the sky, usually the male deity. The Sumerian primordial couple were An, the sky god, and Ki, the earth goddess, and they were in an everlasting embrace. From them came Enlil, the god of air. Enlil separated his parents and married his mother in order to create

Left: This ancient Khmer (Cambodian) bust of Brahma with four faces dates from the late 9th or early 10th century.

humans. For the Maori of New Zealand, Rangi (sky) and Papa (earth) were the primordial couple. They were so tightly embraced with each other that their children had to prize them apart, enabling light to shine on all parts of the world.

Opposite to the separation stories, another common creation theme is the fusing of the male and female primordial couple, who then as one deity perform the act of creation. In Africa the Fon creator deity is half female, Mawu, and half male, Lisa. Mawu symbolizes the moon, night, fertility, and joy. Lisa symbolizes the sun, day, war, and strength. As Mawu-Lisa, the hybrid deity represents the harmony of the universe.

One Chinese myth also features a primordial couple. In the beginning the first humans, Nü and Kua, found

Below: Vishnu, the Hindu creator god who dreamed the world into existence, rests on the serpent of eternity, Ananta, in this 17th-century illustration. The goddess Lakshmi, Vishnu's wife, sits next to the deity.

themselves in the Kunlun Mountains. While offering a burning sacrifice to the gods, the couple prayed for guidance, asking if they, as brother and sister, were meant to be husband and wife. The gods made the smoke from the sacrifice stand still in midair and the couple took this as a sign that they should unite. Nü and Kua then fused together to form a new deity called Nü Kua, who had the head of a woman and the body of a snake. In later myths Nü Kua was the patron of marriage rituals.

Cosmic egg

The cosmic egg as the source of either the world, the first humans, or the creator deity appears in several mythologies around the world. An alternative Chinese creation myth to the story of Nü Kua says that in the beginning there was only an egg. When the egg cracked in two, out of the yoke emerged the giant Panku. The top half of the eggshell formed the sky and the bottom half the earth. After 18,000 years Panku died, and the various parts of his body formed

the sun and moon, the rivers and oceans, and the forests. Finally the fleas that had lived on his body became the ancestors of humans.

The Hindu belief system states that all creation is part of, and exists within, cycles lasting several thousand years. Once one universe is at the end of its cycle and is destroyed, Vishnu, in the form of Brahma, creates a new one from a golden egg. The egg will have the means of creating everything that had existed in the previous universe before its destruction. As the old world sinks in the great flood, the egg will float to the surface of the primordial waters. After Vishnu sleeps for thousands of years, he will awaken as Brahma and crack open the egg to begin the new creation.

A Maori creation myth says that in the beginning the world was covered in water, then one day a large bird flew overhead and dropped a giant egg. The egg cracked when it hit the water and out came the first family of humans, a dog, a pig, and a canoe for them to ride in.

Land from primordial waters

Creator spirits, the world and sky, and sometimes the first humans are occasionally associated with the primordial waters. One Egyptian creation story features the sun god Re, who was fathered by an abyss filled with water. Re rose out of the water, and from his breath came air and the life force (Shu). His saliva was the source of rain and dew and took the form of a goddess (Tefnut). She became his wife and created order in the world. In a Polynesian myth the universe was originally only water. Ku, the creator, used this water to make land and sky.

There is also an aquatic theme to the Norse myth of creation from the epic poem *Völuspá*. The epic explains that a great emptiness existed between the fires of the south and the ice of the north. Over time the two opposites came together in steam that filled the great emptiness. Ymir, a frost giant, then emerged. He was nurtured by milk from a second creature, Audhumla, the primal cow. Ymir was subsequently killed by the gods Odin, Vili, and Vé, who used his body to create the world. His blood became the oceans, his skull the sky, and his teeth the rocks.

Nature as creation metaphor

Another element of creation stories is the use of animals and plants as symbols of life cycles and rebirth. The snake, for example, sheds its skin, and this is widely taken to

Left: The Polynesians, who first inhabited islands such as Bora Bora, shown here, believed that the gods created the world out of the primordial waters.

represent birth or rebirth. It also burrows into the ground (Mother Earth), and it can climb trees, thus reaching the sky, unifying all the elements in creation. Unlike the diabolical serpent in the biblical story of Eden, the snake in other ancient mythologies embodies divinity and accompanies the mother goddess. In statues from Minoan Crete, the mother goddess holds up a snake in each hand. It was believed that the Cretan snakes enhanced the goddess's power and authority, just as the jagged thunderbolts did for Zeus, ruler of the Greek pantheon.

Another symbol of the unification of earth and sky is the primal tree. Yggdrasil, the Norse tree of life, supported the entire universe. One of its roots reached into Asgard, home of the gods; another into Jotunheim, the land of the giants; and a third into Niflheim, the underworld. Yggdrasil

Below: In the center of this Byzantine mosaic from the sixth century CE is a depiction of the earth mother Gaia watching Xanthikos, who symbolizes the month of April. The mosaic is located in Miirata, in Syria.

Kuloskap the Creator

Native American creation stories, which were passed down orally or by song from generation to generation, differ from group to group and depend greatly on location and lifestyle. One example among the warrior cultures of northeastern America, such as the Micmac and Passamaquoddy Indians, is the myth of Kuloskap, the creator. The giant deity brought life, light, and wisdom to his people. He taught them the names of the beings he created, showed them medicinal plants to heal their wounds, and identified foods for them to eat. After his gifts were received by humans, Kuloskap retired to a mountaintop, where he is still said to instruct the young warriors who come to him on their vision quests, spiritual journeys that also represent a rite of passage. A prophetic element is present in myths about Kuloskap, suggesting that in the future, Mother Earth will be renewed and humans will live harmoniously in brotherhood.

represented a world axis or pillar, connecting all creation. The tree, for many mythologies, is both a symbol of wisdom and the origin of humankind. Cultures as diverse as those of ancient Persia and the North American Sioux believed that humanity had been born from a primordial tree.

The creation of humans

In addition to providing an explanation of how the world came into being, many creation myths also tell how the first humans were made. Usually human creation stories include the first humans either being placed on a newly formed world by the supreme creator, or molded, often from clay, by the creator or another, lesser deity. A unique example of molding without clay comes from Aztec mythology. Quetzalcoatl decided he wanted to create the first humans, so he ground up the bones of his dead father and mixed them with his own blood. He then molded the first couple. The Mayan god Huarab tried making people

Below: In many cultures the symbol of a snake with its tail in its mouth symbolized eternity and rebirth. In this drawing, the cosmic turtle and the elephant pillars support the Hindu universe.

from clay, but the material was too soft. He then tried wood, but that was too stupid. He was successful only when he used corn. This myth reflects the importance of corn in Mayan culture.

The treatment meted out by the creator deities to the mythical early humans differed across the world's cultures. Some creator deities were sympathetic to the first humans; others, including those of Sumer, Babylonia, and northern Europe, tended to be largely indifferent to them. Another common occurrence is the divine destruction of most, if not all, early humans, sometimes by a great flood. In these legends, the supreme deities try to eradicate their creations because they have become displeased with human behavior. In Inca mythology, for example, when the supreme deity Viracocha emerged out of nothingness to make the world, he first populated it with giant humans. Before long, however, he became angry with the giants' disobedience and impiety, so he turned them to stone and sent a great flood to cleanse the earth. Once the waters had subsided, Viracocha embarked on his second creation, this time with normal-size humans, whom he taught how to farm and build shelters.

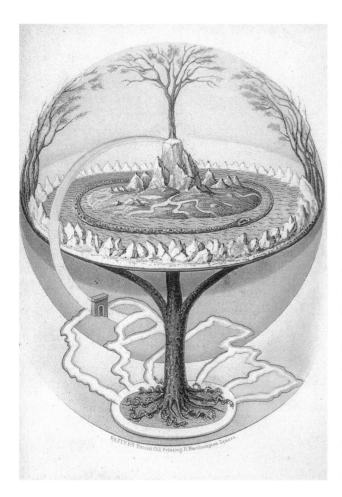

Left: In Norse mythology, the earth was supported by Yggdrasil, the tree of life, the roots of which were in Asgard and the underworld. The heavens were held aloft by its branches.

Revered first couple

A popular myth among the Polynesian cultures is the creation of the first humans by the god Tane. First Tane created a woman. He molded her from red clay. He blew life into her nostrils and named her Hine Ahu One. Tane loved his creation so much that they had a child together, a daughter named Hine Titama. Tane loved her, too, and from their love for each other came the first human couple. All was well until Hine Titama found out that Tane was her father. Disgusted with having unwittingly committed incest, she became the first human to journey to the underworld, thus paving the way for death for all mortals.

The first man and woman often held a place of sacred importance in a particular culture. For example, Kazikamuntu, whose name means "root of man," was the first human of African Banyarwandan mythology. According to the myth he was created by Imana, the chief god. Kazikamuntu had many children, but they argued among each other and left Kazikamuntu's home. Their migration explained the spread of groups and peoples around the world.

Among the Abaluyia peoples of Kenya, it is believed that Mwambu and Sela were the first couple, and that their children colonized the earth. They lived in a house on stilts at a time when the world was populated by monsters. To keep the monsters from invading their home, they would pull up the ladder behind them whenever they returned from an outing. Their children, however, descended to the ground, unafraid of the monsters, and populated the world.

In Norse mythology, it was prophesied that the world of the gods and frost giants would be destroyed in a great apocalypse called Ragnarok. The only survivors would be a human couple, Líf and Leifthrasir, who had taken shelter under Yggdrasil, the world-tree. Once the world was free of giants, it would be repopulated with humans.

BARBARA GARDNER

Bibliography

Hamilton, Virginia. *In the Beginning: Creation Stories from Around the World.* San Diego, CA: Harcourt, 1991.

Leeming, David Adams, and Margaret Adams Leeming. *A Dictionary of Creation Myths.* New York, NY: Oxford University Press, 1996.

SEE ALSO: Africa; Australia; China; Deities; Dualism; Earth Mother; Egypt; Gaia; Great Spirit; Greece; India; Iran; Mesopotamia; Monotheism; Native Americans; Prehistoric Religion; Scandinavia.

A Madagascar Creation Myth

Madagascar is a large island nation off the east coast of Africa, and the cosmogonic myths of the island's indigenous peoples compare the creation of nature to the creation of works of art. In one story, the creator saw his daughter making dolls out of clay. That gave him an idea. He breathed life into them and humans came into being. In another creation story from Madagascar, the creator first made two men and a woman. They each wandered the earth alone, longing for company. One of the two men made a beautiful wooden statue of a woman, which the other man found and fell in love with. The first woman found the statue dressed in flowers by its lover, and took it home with her. When the two men found the woman, all three quarreled over possession of the statue. Taking pity on them, the creator breathed life into the statue, which he said was the child of its maker and the woman who sheltered it. The man who dressed the statue in flowers became the statue-woman's husband, and from them all people are descended. In this ancient myth many later elements are found: the creator gives life to works of art and from their male and female aspects humanity is born.

CRETE

Little is known about the ancient cultures that inhabited the island of Crete from about 6000 BCE. In about 2600 BCE the civilization known as Minoan developed. It reached its peak in about 1600 BCE and then gradually declined between about 1400 and 1100 BCE. Its name comes from the legendary Cretan king, Minos.

Below: According to legend, the eastern slopes of Mount Ida were home to Zeus, who grew up in the cave of Ideon Andron.

Crete, fifth largest of the Mediterranean islands, lies in the Aegean Sea about halfway between Greece and the north coast of Africa. It is nearly 160 miles (257 km) long and 36 miles (58 km) wide, but a mere 6 miles (10 km) at its narrowest point. The island is dominated by its rugged mountains. There are four distinct ranges: the White Mountains in the west, Mount Ida in the center, the Lasithi-Dictean Mountains in the east, and the Sitea range in the far east.

The Minoan sites that have been excavated date back to about 2600 BCE. During the early Minoan period (2600–2000 BCE), trade sprang up between the peoples of Egypt, Asia Minor, and the new inhabitants of Crete. The major industrial development of the time was the discovery of bronze, a strong metal alloy derived from copper and tin. As neither of these metals are found on Crete itself, the widespread use of bronze by the Minoans indicates that trade was common with Cyprus ("island of copper") and with ports farther north and east for tin.

Homer described Crete in the 19th book of his *Odyssey*: "There is a land called Crete, in the midst of the wine-dark sea/A fair rich land, with many men innumerable and 90 cities." Between 2000 and 1700 BCE, the Minoans built great palaces at Knossos, Phaistos, Mallia, and Kato Zakro. Archaeologists have also found evidence of towns and villages whose buildings resemble those of the big palaces, only in miniature.

Earthquakes are common in the Aegean. In the 1600s BCE one shook the island of Thera, just before the largest volcanic eruption the world had ever known. In about 1628 the center of Thera vanished suddenly into the sea.

Archaeologists working on Thera (now named Santorini for a fourth-century saint) originally thought that the volcanic eruption occurred in the 1400s BCE and was responsible for the destruction of the Minoan civilization. However, more recent work has shown that the Minoans recovered from the devastating flooding caused by the tsunami that rushed south from Thera and the ash that darkened the sky and covered the land.

Settlements on Crete were rebuilt and the palaces were restored in even greater magnificence. Between 1600 and 1425 BCE, these palace-cities reflected the increasing wealth of their inhabitants: wealth displayed in the beauty of their homes and the quality of their lives as revealed by the frescoed walls and exquisitely made artifacts. The Minoans did not display their power in martial form. Unusually for the time, the Minoan palaces stood without fortification walls, without protective moats, and without lookout towers. Those who ruled from Knossos and the other palaces were secure in their homes and on the seas. According to Thucydides (*History* 1.4), Minos was the first ruler to establish a navy. He made himself master of what is now known as the Hellenic Sea, colonizing and ruling over the Cyclades.

Minoan religion

Although the rulers of the palace-cities were male, the principal Minoan deity was probably a Mother Goddess. She may have been a fertility figure, taking on a variety of forms associated with animals and vegetation. Alternatively these forms may have been separate goddesses. It is likely that the goddess was served by priestesses, although the palace rulers may have played an important religious role.

The Minoans practiced their cults both outside their homes and within them. The rugged landscape of Crete gave rise to some of their religious practices: both caves and mountain peaks inspired religious awe and were often sites for sanctuaries. The design of their palaces and houses included areas for religious rituals and practices.

Above: Pillars were sacred to the Minoans. This pillar at the palace of Phaistos is decorated with the sacred double-ax symbol.

Zeus and the cave in Mount Dicte

According to the earliest Greek myths about the Olympian gods, Crete played an important part in the early life of Zeus, king of the gods. Cronus, son of the two original beings, Uranus and Gaia, married his sister Rhea. He was warned, either by the Moirai (Fates), Gaia, or Uranus (according to different versions of the story), that he would be overthrown by his own child. To prevent this from happening, Cronus swallowed each of his children at birth.

When Rhea was pregnant with her sixth child, she turned to Gaia for help and they concocted a plan. After the baby was born, Rhea wrapped a stone in a swaddling blanket and gave it to her husband to gulp down. She then took her newborn son to Crete and hid him in a cave on either Mount Dicte or Mount Ida, according to different versions of the myth. There bees brought him honey, and the goat Amaltheia brought him milk. The Curetes (young men) clashed their spears on their shields to drown out the baby's cries. When Zeus grew to maturity, he forced Cronus to regurgitate his brothers and sisters. With the help of the Cyclopes and the Hundred-Handed Ones, Zeus and his siblings overthrew Cronus after a long, desperate battle.

Origin of the Cretans

Greek myth traces the origin of the inhabitants of Crete to the story of Zeus and Europa. According to this legend, Zeus came to Europa, a princess of Tyre, in the form of an attractive white bull. The princess soon noticed the playful animal and began to deck his horns with garlands. Zeus lured Europa to climb on his back and then leaped into the sea. He swam to Crete, coming ashore near Gortyn. There he revealed his true identity and intentions, and lay with the maiden in a willow thicket by a spring—or, as a later version tells it, under an evergreen plane tree, which was shown as "the very spot" for many years. From the union of god and princess were born the three legendary kings of Crete: Minos, Rhadamanthys, and Sarpedon. Minos played an important role in the best-known myth about Crete, that of Theseus and the Minotaur.

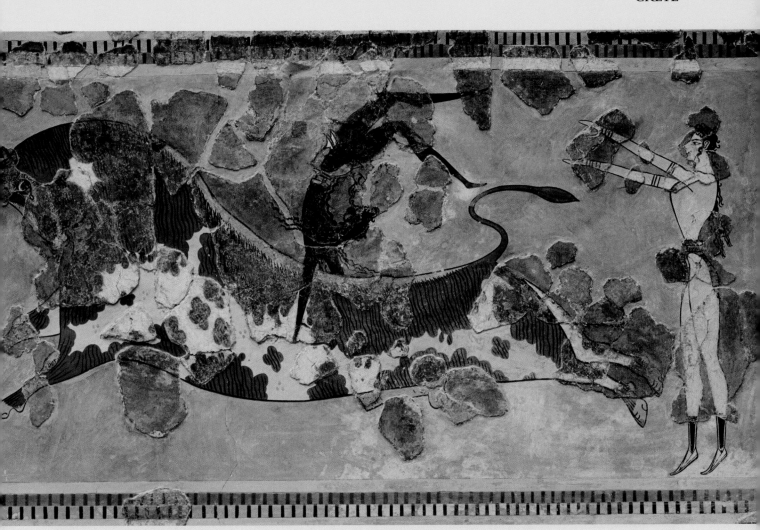

Theseus and the Minotaur

Theseus was born to Aethra in Troezen. Aethra's father, the
king of Troezen, declared that Aegeus, king of Athens, was
the baby's father, but Aethra said that his father was the sea
god Poseidon. Whatever the truth, Theseus himself gained
benefits from both his mortal and his immortal father.

When Aegeus left Troezen, he placed a sword and a pair
of sandals beneath a heavy rock and told Aethra that when
her son could lift the stone, he should take the tokens and
make his way to Athens.

When he came of age, Theseus retrieved the sword and
sandals and made his way north along the Gulf of Corinth.
Along his route he encountered a series of local brigands
who preyed upon all travelers. Theseus quickly eliminated
these cruel men, in each case using their own method of
execution against them. Procrustes, for instance, forced
anyone he captured to lie in a special bed. He then
stretched or chopped his victim to fit the bed. Theseus
did the same to him. Today philosophers still use the
phrase "Procrustes' bed" when shaping an argument to
fit a favorite theory.

*Above: The famous bull-leaping fresco from the palace at Knossos. It
shows the three stages of a successful leap over the beast's horns.*

Upon reaching Athens, Theseus went to Aegeus's palace.
The king recognized the sword and sandals and welcomed
the young man as his son and heir to the throne.

The son of Minos, the king of Crete, had been insulted
(or killed) in Athens. In recompense, Minos demanded an
annual gift of seven boys and seven girls, whom he fed to
the Minotaur, a monster with the body of a man and the
head, horns, and tail of a bull. The Minotaur had been born
to Minos's wife Pasiphae, who had coupled with a white
bull that Poseidon had sent to be used as a sacrifice and
which Minos had kept instead. The horrified king had kept
the Minotaur hidden. He asked the craftsman Daedalus to
build a labyrinth, a vast maze so cleverly planned that
anyone who ventured in would be unable to find his way
out again. The Minotaur was imprisoned at the center.

In the third year of the tribute payment, Theseus
volunteered, or was chosen, to lead the expedition to
Crete. He promised his father that, if he killed the

Atlantis

The lost island of Atlantis has given rise to centuries of speculation. According to legend, Atlantis was a rich and powerful island that was swallowed up by the sea as a result of earthquakes. People have claimed to have discovered the lost civilization in many parts of the world. One of the most popular versions connects Atlantis with the island of Thera (Santorini).

The ancient Greek philosopher Plato described a civilization that sounds very much like that of the Minoans. According to his dialogue *Critias*, Atlantis vanished suddenly, destroyed in the space of a night and a day. The event has a parallel in history. In about 1628 BCE, the center of Thera exploded after a powerful earthquake. It was the largest volcanic eruption in the world's history. A 60-foot (18-m) tidal wave rushed south to smash against Crete. Ash darkened the sun. This ash was carried around the world: there are reports of it in every civilization, and tree rings in the western United States record its effects.

The rim of the volcano is now the modern island of Santorini. The volcanic basin, known as a caldera, became flooded by the Aegean Sea. The sea in the caldera is so deep that divers cannot reach its bottom. No shipwrecks or bodies have been found in the waters within the island's shell.

In the 1960s archaeologists began excavations on the island. They discovered the remains of a rich and beautiful civilization, very much like that on Crete. While scholars now know that the destruction of Thera did not cause the final downfall of Crete itself, they also know that the island must have been part of the Minoan empire. The many parallels between Plato's account and the history of Minoan Crete and surrounding islands provide compelling evidence that Thera gave rise to the legend of Atlantis, lost forever in a natural explosion.

Below: The modern town of Thera is perched on the edge of the caldera on the west coast of Santorini.

Minotaur and returned unharmed, he would change the ship's black sail to white, so that Aegeus would know that his son still lived.

An incident on the voyage to Crete showed that Theseus enjoyed the support of his immortal father, Poseidon. The Cretan ambassador tossed a ring overboard and dared Theseus to retrieve it. The young prince leaped into the sea. In its depths he was welcomed by Amphitrite, wife of Poseidon, and other sea nymphs and given a magnificent crown. Everyone was amazed when Theseus returned safely to the surface bearing a star-studded crown.

At Knossos, Theseus won the attention of the princess Ariadne. She gave him a ball of thread to unwind as he made his way through the labyrinth to the Minotaur at its center. Theseus confronted the creature and killed it. Then, retracing his steps using the thread, he made his way safely out of the palace. Theseus set sail for Athens, taking Ariadne with him.

Theseus stopped at the first island he came across, Naxos. He set sail again without Ariadne. Some say that he chose to abandon her, others that he acted on the command of the gods. He had, however, given her the crown from the nymphs of the sea. Dionysus, one of the 12 Olympian gods, saw the lonely princess, rescued her, and put the crown into the sky, where it became the constellation now known as Corona, the crown.

When he returned to Athens, Theseus forgot the promise he had made to his father and did not hoist a white sail. When Aegeus saw the dark sails, he assumed that his son was dead and threw himself into the sea in despair. Ever since, the sea has been called the Aegean Sea.

Theseus then became king of Athens. He made the city strong and prosperous, and he became known for his wisdom and compassion.

The liberation of Athens by Theseus from its tribute to Crete is a myth. However, historians know that the people of mainland Greece, the Mycenaeans, took over the Minoan civilization on Crete in about 1400 BCE. So the legend of Theseus and the Minotaur may reflect historical events.

Legend and archaeology

British archaeologist Sir Arthur Evans came to Crete in 1903 because he believed that there was some truth behind the famous legend of King Minos, his great palace at Knossos, and the labyrinth beneath it. Evans planned to stay for only a year or two, but his findings were so exciting and extensive that he continued to excavate at the Palace of King Minos (as he called it) for the next 40 years. Excavations still continue at this site of the largest and most magnificent of the Minoan palaces. With its 1,200 rooms

Right: A faience (glazed pottery) figure of the snake goddess found at the palace of Knossos. She is wearing typical Minoan dress.

more stories. Broad stairways led to the upper rooms. Both lower and upper halls could be left open to the sun and air or closed off by folding doors built across them. Windows, perhaps paned with thin sheets of alabaster, brought light into the rooms from the exterior of the palace.

In the lowest part of the building, large square columns marked off what archaeologists call "pillar crypts." The Minoans carved the sacred symbol of the double ax on these pillars and placed offering bowls next to them. It is thought that it was here the people celebrated the ties between heaven and earth and perhaps thanked their deities for the continued security of their palace in a region often shaken by earthquakes.

In small rooms off the central court and in the southwest part of the palace, another type of cult was celebrated. It is here that the famous figurines of women holding and encircled by snakes were found. They are usually identified as "snake goddesses," but they could also be priestesses celebrating rites with sacred snakes.

Many cultures believed that the serpent was a magical animal and associated it with rebirth. The snake can live above ground and below it, and it seems to be reborn each spring when it sheds its old skin and appears in a bright new one. Its worship in Greece continued from the Minoan through the classical period.

Scattered throughout the palace at Knossos are small lowered rooms to which one descends by a series of turning steps. The rooms are lined with thin sheets of alabaster, and a column stands at the turn of the steps. Evans called these rooms "lustral basins," but their purpose is not known. As they are in both public and private areas, it is tempting to suggest they may have had more than one purpose. Cults could be practiced here, but so could simple bathing. All that is known for certain is that these small recessed rooms are found in all the palaces.

and its vast system of winding corridors, the palace resembled a labyrinth. It is quite possible that it provided the basis for the myth.

The palace-cities and religion

The design of the palaces at Knossos, Phaistos, Mallia, and Kato Zakro share a similar layout, a similar structural design, similar units of measure, and a similar style of interior decoration. Even the smaller residences, such as Aghia Triada, Tylissos, Mochlos, and Palaikastro look like the larger palace-cities. The great house at Gournia also boasts features similar to those at the palaces.

Archaeologists believe that these palace-cities were centers of political, economic, and religious activity. The layout of the palace-city was unusual. The rooms seem to have been built outward from a central courtyard, a large rectangular space always oriented north-south. Opening upon the courtyard were large halls, usually having two or

The maze

The word *labyrinth* comes from *labys*, the name given to the double ax. This double-bladed weapon is carved in stylized form on many pillars within the palaces and adorns vases. Placed in specially designed stands, the double ax stood guard before the storerooms that housed the palace's wealth. Many scholars believe that the *labys* played a role in the Minoans' religion. Like many of the recurrent artifacts and symbols, the double ax may have played a dual role as a weapon and a cult object.

The Minoans designed their palaces in a mazelike pattern. Passageways are never straight but turn inward from the front entrances to the central court. Anyone not familiar with the layout of the palace could easily get lost in the many halls and rooms. This labyrinthine design may have served a religious purpose. Certainly the labyrinth design was transferred from the Cretan palaces to the entrances of Gothic churches, where it represented the maze of life. In churches, however, the figure of the Minotaur, pictured at the labyrinth's center in early myth and art, was replaced with an image of Jerusalem. Even today, Christian churches are sometimes built with a labyrinth pattern on the floor, so people can walk its passageways and meditate upon their steps in the maze of life.

Minoan cults

The Minoans worshiped their deities with rituals performed at the palaces, and archaeologists have suggested several types of cults. Most seem to have involved offerings, probably sacrifices of animals such as bulls. As frescoes and vase designs reveal, these sacrifices were accompanied by dancing and song.

The central cult involved boldly performed bull-dancing rituals. Archaeologists have assumed that they played a religious role and were not merely a sport. The later Greek athletic contests took place in honor of the gods, so it seems likely that this was also true of the Minoans. The earliest Greek myths feature Zeus as a bull, and the celebration of the bull seems to stand at the center of Minoan religion. Although the pillar cults and rites celebrated within caves were probably dark and mysterious, there generally seems to have been a sense of joy in the Minoan religion (see box, right).

There is evidence that, at least on one occasion, Minoan ceremonies took a more serious turn and required a different sort of sacrifice. At Archanes, the first (and so far only) evidence of human sacrifice in Crete was discovered. It was uncovered first by Evans and then extensively excavated by a Greek team under the direction of Yianni and Efi Sakellarakis. In a temple there stood an altar. On the altar was the body of an 18-year-old male. The skeletons of a priest with a knife and a priestess with a bowl were found nearby. It seems that an earthquake collapsed the sanctuary building just before the sacrifice was to take place. This was followed by a fire caused by one of the many oil lamps in the sanctuary. Perhaps the sacrifice was intended as a last desperate offering to the gods to avert an expected disaster.

Minoan Bull Cult

The bull was sacred to many early civilizations. It was a symbol of strength and fertility. Bull gods were worshiped in Sumeria, Egypt, and India. The bull has a central role in the Greek myths based around Crete, and as a result, many people believe that the bull played a vital role in Minoan cults. Frescoes and statuettes seem to indicate that the Minoans were skilled in bull-jumping. In this sport, a youth or maiden grasped the horns of the bull and vaulted, or somersaulted, over its back. Archaeologists believe that bull-leaping may have been practiced in the central courtyard of the palace at Knossos. It is possible that the bull was sacrificed at the end. Bull-jumping may have been part sport, part ritual, and part entertainment. It certainly tested the participants' courage and skill.

In addition to frescoes and statues of bulls, stylized bull horns adorned the palace roofs, and vases and cups in the shape of bull's heads have been found during excavation. The place between the bull horns formed small altars for offerings to the gods, both in the palaces and in mountain shrines. It is likely that the Minoans saw the bull's horns as a symbol of its strength.

Right: This libation vessel was carved from black steatite. The horns of gilded wood have been restored.

Minoan Deities

Religion played an important role in Minoan life, but all our information about it is based on artifacts. They suggest that Minoan religion was based on agriculture and fertility and that goddesses were more important than gods. However, it is uncertain whether the Minoans believed in one goddess who took many forms or several goddesses. Everything in the world seemed to have a religious meaning, particularly trees, stone pillars, and springs. Sanctuaries were in caves and on the tops of hills and mountains. Most priests were women, although the palace kings may have had some religious functions.

Earth Goddess: Goddess of fertility, animals, harvests, households, and the underworld.

Snake Goddess: Identity and function uncertain: may be an aspect of the Earth goddess or a separate divinity.

Mistress of Animals: Protectress of animals and the natural world.

Demons: Humans with hands but lions' feet; servants of the gods.

Above: In The Minotaur *(1885), English artist George Frederic Watts (1817–1904) emphasizes the loneliness of the creature.*

Above: The Rape of Europa *by Maerten de Vos (1531–1603) shows Zeus in the form of a bull abducting the princess of Tyre. According to legend, the rape resulted in Europa's giving birth to three kings of Crete.*

Cave and mountain sanctuaries

The cave on Mount Dicte can still be visited today. It is possible to descend into its depths and see where, according to legend, the baby Zeus lay amid the subterranean stalactites and stalagmites. The huge cave in Mount Ida can also be visited by modern tourists. Since both places claimed to be the birthplace of Zeus, it is probable that they were rivals. Both were certainly important places for cult worship.

In the late 1980s, archaeologists working at Palaikastro found a statue of a youthful god. Although it lacks any inscription to give it a secure identification, many scholars believe that it represents Zeus in his youth before he ascended to Mount Olympus.

The caves of Zeus are not the only ones thought to be significant in Minoan religion. Many caves seem to have been sites where the Minoans practiced a cult that celebrated the gods and goddesses who made their land fertile. Numerous votive offerings have been found in them in the form of animals such as sheep, goats, bulls, and even a large cache of turtles.

Minoans also worshiped their gods on the mountains. Peak sanctuaries have been found throughout the island, and models of these have been found in archaeological sites. On the mountaintops, altars in the form of stylized bull horns marked where cave sanctuaries were located; the bull horns topped the peak sanctuary building as well. No one knows, however, what form the rituals at these caves and peak sanctuaries took.

KARELISA HARTIGAN

Bibliography

Farnaux, Alexandre, and David J. Baker, trans. *Knossos: Searching for the Legendary Palace of King Minos.* New York: Harry N. Abrams, 1996.
Macgillivray, Joseph Alexander. *Minotaur: Sir Arthur Evans and the Archaeology of the Minoan Myth.* New York: Hill and Wang, 2000.

SEE ALSO: Animal-headed Figures; Flood Myths; Greece; Minos; Natural Forces; Theseus.

CRONUS

In Greek mythology Cronus was the youngest of the Titan children of the creator deities Uranus and Gaia. He dethroned his father as ruler of the universe but was himself overthrown by his own mighty children, the Olympians, led by Zeus.

The creation story in Greek mythology begins with Uranus (Heaven or Sky) fertilizing Gaia (Earth) by raining on her. As Uranus's wife, Gaia then gave birth to many beings, most important the one-eyed giants named the Cyclopes; worker giants called the Hecatoncheires, each with a hundred hands; and the humanoid Titans, which were a primeval race of intelligent giants. Cronus was the youngest Titan.

Uranus grew jealous of his children and, according to Hesiod's *Theogony*, written in the eighth century BCE, he forced them back into the body of Gaia. The pain of having to carry her grown children inside her was too great for Gaia, and she called on them for help in overthrowing Uranus. Only Cronus was brave enough to volunteer. Gaia released Cronus, who armed himself with a sickle and hid when his father next visited his mother. At the right moment Cronus castrated Uranus and threw his genitals into the sea. According to one source, out of the foam produced by Uranus's genitals grew Aphrodite, goddess of love and beauty. Rendered powerless, Uranus relinquished his throne to Cronus, but not before warning him that he too would be defeated by one of his own children.

As the new ruler of the universe, Cronus freed the other Titans, the Cyclopes, and the Hecatoncheires and married his sister Rhea. He soon grew convinced, however, that the others were intent on removing him from power, so he imprisoned them again, despite Gaia's protests.

Left: Saturn Devouring a Son (about 1636), by Flemish painter Peter Paul Rubens, was commissioned by King Philip IV of Spain for his royal hunting lodge. Saturn was the Roman name for Cronus.

Cronus's paranoia was not abated by imprisoning his siblings, and when Rhea became pregnant, Cronus recalled Uranus's final warning. Rhea was about to give birth to the first Olympian, Hestia, who would become the goddess of the hearth. As soon as Hestia was born Cronus snatched her away from Rhea and swallowed her whole. When Rhea was next pregnant, this time with the goddess Demeter, Cronus again swallowed the newborn baby. Three more times Rhea gave birth and Cronus devoured the children in order to eliminate any threat to his power.

When Rhea was pregnant for the sixth time, she turned to Gaia for help, and the two came up with a scheme to save the next baby. First Rhea hid from Cronus—some sources say that she sought refuge in a cave on the island of Crete; others claim that she went to the rough hill country of Arcadia—and gave birth to Zeus. She then handed the baby to two nymph sisters, Adrasteia and Ida, who would nourish him on the milk from Amaltheia, a goat deity. Once Rhea knew her baby was safe, she wrapped a stone in swaddling clothes, returned to Cronus, and gave it to him. Thinking it was the newborn baby, he swallowed it. It has been suggested by historians that the subjugation of Rhea to Cronus and of Gaia to Uranus reflects the more malevolent, sky-god traditions of peoples who over centuries gradually invaded mainland Greece and merged uneasily with the region's earlier inhabitants.

Zeus's revenge

When Zeus grew up, he and Rhea devised a plan for rescuing his siblings. Together they made Cronus's favorite honeyed drink, but secretly added mustard and salt to it. When he gulped it down, the sickening mixture made him vomit. He heaved up the stone he had thought was his last child; then he vomited up the other five children, who by now were fully grown.

These children, the Olympians, immediately declared war on Cronus. Zeus and his siblings joined forces with many of the Cyclopes and Hecatoncheires. Cronus had powerful allies too. Most of the Titans and the river goddess Styx sided with him. The Cyclopes fashioned thunder and lightning into potent weapons for Zeus.

The war raged for a decade before Cronus was finally deposed and banished with his Titan allies. Some say they were imprisoned in the underworld realm of Tartarus, guarded by the Hecatoncheires. Roman writer Plutarch

Right: Saturn Devouring One of His Children (1821–1823), by the Spanish painter Francisco Goya (1746–1828), was most likely based on the 17th-century painting by Rubens (opposite).

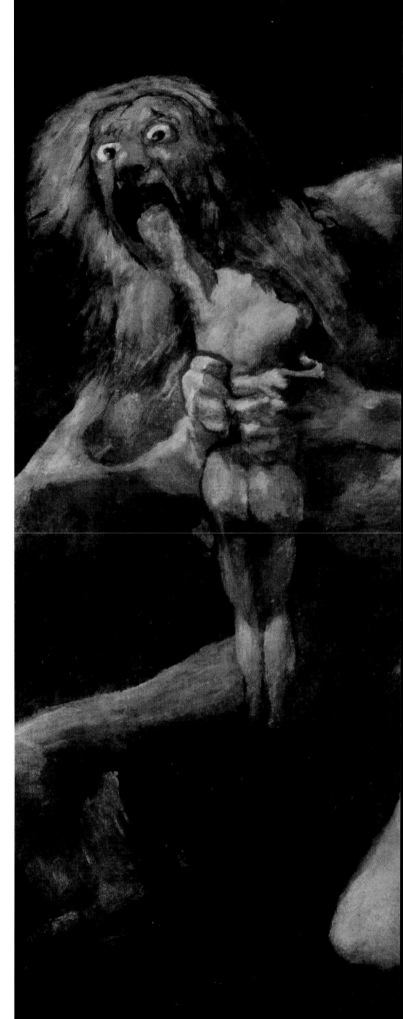

In the engraving: POLIDORO DA CARAVAGGIO INVENTORE

Gio. Bat. Galestruzzi fece 1

Above: This 17th-century engraving is copied from an artwork depicting Uranus being castrated by his son Cronus. Gaia, Uranus's wife and the mother of Cronus, stands behind Cronus.

(c. 46–120 CE), however, wrote that Cronus was banished to the Isle of the Blessed, near Britain. Other accounts state that Zeus made Cronus ruler of Elysium, the fabled place where the souls of dead heroes lived.

Cronus and the Golden Age

There are some versions that depict the reign of Cronus as a golden age when all creatures lived in harmony with nature and each other. This different depiction of Cronus may have come from an ancient pre-Greek Cronus who was a grain deity in an era when wars were less common. The ancient Greeks believed that the Golden Age was a benevolent time for mortals, where there was no need for swords or weapons of any kind, abusive language was never spoken, and neither punishment nor retribution were ever considered. Even animals were kind to each other. It was a time when the universe revolved backward and the world was a paradise of abundance, where streams flowed full of milk and honey, and no one knew hunger. In many ways the Golden Age of Cronus was similar to the biblical Garden of Eden.

During the reign of Cronus, women did not give birth; humans rose out of the earth, and were thus said to be autochthonous. Because no one had parents, there were naturally no families. The humans of the Golden Age not only talked to each other but also spoke to and learned from all kinds of animals. Although the autochthons were

The Olympians' Revulsion at Eating Children

Cronus was not the only character in Greek mythology who ate his own children. There are other Greek myths in which a father serves up his children as a horrifying meal for others. The most infamous of these stories was that of Tantalus, a wealthy king who was said to be a son of Zeus. He was popular with the Olympian deities and frequently dined with them. One day, wondering if they were as all-knowing as they claimed to be, Tantalus had his infant son Pelops butchered and made into a stew. Then he invited the gods to dinner.

The goddess Demeter, still dazed with grief over the loss of her daughter Persephone to Hades, barely realized what she was doing when she began to eat. The other gods shrank back in shock and revulsion, for they had immediately understood the nature of the meat. They swiftly restored the poor infant to life and, since Demeter had already swallowed the tiny left shoulder blade, they replaced it with ivory. As for Tantalus, the gods sent him to the depths of gloomy Tartarus, where he remained "tantalizingly" (the word comes from his name) close to a refreshing pool of water and perfectly ripe, juicy fruits. Thus, the punishment of Tantalus was to go mad with thirst and hunger in the middle of an abundance he could never have. The severity of the punishment indicates the revulsion felt by the Olympians in the face of such child abuse. This is all the more understandable when one remembers that they too had been victims of such abuse by Cronus.

mortal, for them death came like a pleasant sleep without pain or fear.

The Golden Age ended when Zeus defeated Cronus. In one version of the fate of Cronus that relates to the story of the Golden Age, Cronus was placed by Zeus in a secret place where he lay sleeping, protected by women until the time was right for him to wake again and reign over another golden age.

Origins of Cronus

Most scholars agree that *Cronus* is a pre-Greek word, but where it came from is less clear. There is also disagreement concerning the origins of the character of Cronus. One speculation is that the Greek Cronus was adapted from the Phoenician god Moloch, who also devoured children.

Another theory is that Cronus may have been a pre-Greek deity who taught people the use of honey and was connected with grain. Evidence for this comes in part from the only important ritual associated with him in Greek times, the Cronia, a July harvest festival honoring Cronus and Rhea. The festival was held mainly in Athens; in Thebes, where it included a music contest; and on the island of Rhodes. It was a lively celebration that blurred social distinctions between master and slave and placed all celebrants on an equal footing. Evidence from Rhodes suggests that the ritual may have included human sacrifice. There was an instance when a condemned criminal, drugged with wine, was sacrificed outside the city gates at the shrine of Artemis Aristobule.

Right: This Roman sculpture depicts the moment when Rhea gives Cronus a rock wrapped in a blanket, which he believes to be the infant Zeus. Cronus swallows the rock without noticing the trick.

In addition to the Cronia, a ritual was held every spring in Athens, during which Cronus was honored with a sacrificial cake. At the spring equinox in Olympia, his priests offered sacrifices on a nearby hill named for him, and in summertime the people of Cyrene wore crowns of fresh figs and celebrated Cronus as the vegetation god who had taught them about fruits and honey.

Wars among the gods

Incidents of deities fighting each other, episodes known as cosmic wars, such as the usurpation of Uranus by Cronus and the battle between Cronus and his children the Olympians, are frequently found in world mythologies.

Above: The infant Zeus being secretly raised by the nymphs and reared on milk from the goat deity Amaltheia. According to legend, when Zeus dethroned Cronus and became ruler of the gods, he showed his thanks to the goat by making her the star Capella in the constellation Auriga.

Such struggles are usually interpreted as evidence of an older culture or religious tradition whose adherents were often demonized by the usurping, new culture or religion. For example, in addition to the cosmic wars of Greek myth, similar battles occur in ancient myths of India between the *ashuras* (demons), who were identified by their mothers' surnames, and their younger siblings, the *devas* (shining ones), gods who were identified by their fathers' surnames. The battles between the *ashuras* and the *devas* have been seen by some scholars as a metaphor for the historical conflict between an older, matriarchal culture in parts of India and an invading patriarchal culture.

Similarly, Celtic mythology includes the story of the Battle of Moytura, where an ancient race of dark, brutal, misshapen giants called the Fomorii were defeated by invading, handsome deities known as the Tuatha De Danaan. Another example, from Babylonian mythology, is the battle between the mother of the gods, an evil she-dragon named Tiamat, and the young champion deity called Marduk. Tiamat tried to destroy the gods but Marduk defeated her. After his victory Marduk was made the chief deity of the Babylonian pantheon. In Aztec mythology the young god of war, Huitzilopochtli, defeated his older warrior sister, Coyolxauhqui, and 400 brothers.

Cronus in art

The Romans adopted many of the characteristics and stories of Cronus for their ancient Italian deity Saturn, and because of the impact that the Roman empire had on the Western world, many Greek myths and characters that became the subject of works of art were titled by their Roman names. Perhaps the most famous painting of Cronus or Saturn is *Saturn Devouring One of His Children* by Francisco Goya (1746–1828), Spain's most influential artist of the late 18th and early 19th centuries. By the mid-1780s Goya had become one of the leading painters at the royal court in Madrid, where he studied many of the Old Masters.

Cronus, Philyra, and Cheiron

Cronus mated not only with Rhea. He also had a child with a young water maiden named Philyra, one of the countless daughters of Cronus's eldest Titan brother, Oceanus. Philyra was unwilling to be part of such a union with her uncle and fled. Cronus changed himself into a stallion and raced after her. When he caught her they mated, and the infant she bore was the centaur Cheiron, part horse and part man.

Appalled by a child she found hideous, Philyra begged the gods to free her from having to rear such an abomination. They heard her pleas and changed her into a peaceful, honey-sweet linden (lime) tree. The young Cheiron was emotionally wounded by his mother's desertion. He could have turned angry and belligerent, like the other centaurs, but instead he grew up to be gentle, caring, and wise in the arts of medicine, music, herbs, ethics, and archery.

Stepbrother to the Olympians, Cheiron was perhaps the wisest of them all. He became a surrogate parent and teacher to boys who grew up to be among Greece's greatest mythic heroes, including Heracles, the physician Asclepius, Achilles, Jason, Aeneas, and others. Even the god Apollo is said to have been his student for a brief time.

In another version Philyra did not detest her son, nor was she transformed into a linden tree. Instead she lived with Cheiron in his cave on Mount Pelion, enjoying her son's kindness and wisdom. Cheiron was eventually made into the constellation Sagittarius by Zeus.

Above: This painting by Italian artist Parmigianino (1503–1540) shows Cronus transformed into a horse to catch Philyra.

Some art historians believe that Goya's inspiration for his painting of Saturn was an early 17th-century painting of the same subject by the great Flemish artist Peter Paul Rubens (1577–1640). Around 1636, Rubens, who was a favorite of the kings of both Spain and England, was commissioned by King Philip IV of Spain to paint some 60 oil sketches based on Ovid's *Metamorphoses*. Despite his old age and ill health, Rubens completed the commission within a couple of years, and the paintings were hung at the Torre de la Parada, the royal hunting lodge outside Madrid. His *Saturn Devouring a Son* is from that series.

Comparing masterpieces

Although both Goya's and Rubens's paintings of Saturn eating his child are disturbing, each treats the subject matter differently. Rubens's Saturn is a one-dimensional monster who appears as if he were out on a stroll and had stopped momentarily to wolf down a child in the same way that he might wolf down a pastry. There is anguish in the painting, which comes solely from the face of the poor child.

Goya's *Saturn*, on the other hand, is far more complicated and nightmarish. Toward the end of his life, when the painting was made, Goya was profoundly deaf, a widower, and had retired from public life. During this lonely time he painted for his own home a series of works that have little tonal contrast and are overwhelmingly dark in color and theme. The series is known as Goya's "black paintings," of which *Saturn* is the most famous. Many interpretations have been applied to the painting, from a political commentary on Spain during the Napoleonic era to a lament for the death of the artist's own children—his wife had numerous miscarriages and stillbirths, leaving only one son surviving out of around 20 pregnancies—yet no definitive explanation exists. What is clear is that Goya's *Saturn* is not without emotion. By covering the lower portion of his face, it is arguable that the eyes of Saturn express very human emotions such as pain, shock, and despair. As with all truly great art, Goya's *Saturn* allows viewers to see a part of themselves in the painting, a part some viewers might rather leave unacknowledged.

KATHLEEN JENKS

Bibliography

Hesiod, and Richard Lattimore, trans. *Hesiod: The Work and Days, Theogony, and the Shield of Herakles.* Ann Arbor, MI: University of Michigan Press, 1991.

Howatson, M.C., and Ian Chilvers. *Concise Oxford Companion to Classical Literature.* New York: Oxford University Press, 1993.

SEE ALSO: Aphrodite; Blood; Creation Myths; Demeter; Furies; Gaia; Greece; Hestia; Oceanus; Saturn; Titans; Uranus; Zeus.

CUPID

Cupid was the Roman god of love. Also known as Amor, he was the Roman counterpart of the Greek god Eros. His name was derived from the Latin *cupido*, meaning "desire."

Cupid was the son of Venus, goddess of love. Some accounts give his father as Mercury, the winged messenger of the gods, while others say that Cupid was the result of Venus's love affair with Mars, god of war. The Romans usually depicted him as a winged child, or baby, carrying a bow and a quiver full of arrows. He was also occasionally depicted as a beautiful adolescent, with or without wings. Sometimes he was shown wearing armor. This may be a reference to his paternity, or to draw a parallel between warfare and love, or to suggest the invincible power of love.

From his birth Cupid was an essential part of Venus's retinue, firing his arrows to inflame both men and women with passion. Since Venus (the Roman counterpart of the Greek goddess Aphrodite) was a notoriously jealous and spiteful goddess, it is not surprising that Cupid was portrayed as a willful and mischievous child, delighting in the complications that sometimes arise from sudden passion. However, unlike his mother, he was more often playful than malicious, although in some stories he did show a spiteful side.

According to the Roman poet Horace, Cupid's arrows were sharpened on a grindstone dampened with blood. In myth, Cupid had two different kinds of arrows. His leaden arrows filled their target with a fugitive, sensual desire that merely needed to be satisfied, while his golden arrows inspired a more spiritual and lasting love. In Shakespeare's play *A Midsummer Night's Dream*, Hermia makes a promise to her lover Lysander: "I swear to thee, by Cupid's strongest bow,/By his best arrow with the golden head,/By the simplicity of Venus' doves,/By that which knitteth souls and prospers loves."

Left: Cupid (1807) by Denis-Antoine Chaudet (1763–1810) holds a butterfly by its wings. The butterfly may symbolize Psyche or the torment Cupid brings to the human soul.

Cupid is a Romanized version of the Greek god Eros, but he lacks much of the latter's elemental energy. According to Hesiod's *Theogony*, Eros was present at the creation of the world and was one of the first beings. For the Greeks, therefore, Eros was not just the god of sensual or romantic love, he was also a primordial force without which life itself was not possible. This Greek sense of the immense power of Eros as a creative principle, which could wreak havoc as easily as it brings harmony, is almost entirely absent from the figure of Cupid as imagined in Roman and later times.

Cupid and Psyche

The most famous myth about Cupid is the tale of Cupid and Psyche, as told by the Roman writer Lucius Apuleius (c. 124–c. 170 CE) in his *Metamorphoses* (also known as *The Golden Ass*).

Psyche was one of three daughters of a king and queen. All three were fair, but Psyche's beauty was so astonishing that people flocked to marvel at her and sing her praises. As they did so they forgot to worship Venus, and her temples and altars were neglected. The goddess was enraged and determined to punish Psyche for her presumption. She called her son Cupid and ordered him to punish Psyche by making her fall in love with an unworthy being. However, when Cupid saw Psyche he was so struck by her beauty that he fell in love with her himself.

Psyche's two sisters married, but Psyche remained single. It seemed that, while everyone admired her, no mortal fell in love with her. This distressed both Psyche and her parents. They consulted an oracle who told them to take her to the top of a high mountain, where a monster would take her for its wife. Although her parents were devastated, Psyche decided to submit to her fate.

As she waited fearfully for the monster to arrive, she was lifted into the air by Zephyr, the west wind, who placed her in a flowery grove, where she fell asleep. On waking, she discovered that she was near a marvelous palace, which was far richer and more beautiful than any earthly one.

A disembodied voice spoke in her ear. It told her that the palace belonged to her and that invisible servants would obey all her commands. After bathing and eating, she went to bed. In the night someone whom she knew was her husband came to her, but she could not see him. Night after night her husband continued to come, but he always arrived in the dark and left before dawn.

Psyche fell in love and begged her husband to reveal himself to her. He refused, asking why she needed to see him: did she doubt his love? Psyche was calmed, but despite

Cupid and Ovid

There are numerous references to Cupid and his escapades in Latin poetry and literature. The great poet Ovid, writing at the time of Emperor Augustus (63 BCE–14 CE), features Cupid in his witty and cynical manual of seduction, *The Art of Love*, and in his famous poem *Metamorphoses*.

In *The Art of Love* Cupid is characterized as a willful child: "Cupid indeed is obstinate and wild,/A stubborn god; but yet the god's a child:/Easy to govern in his tender age."

In *Metamorphoses* Cupid plays a crucial role in Ovid's version of the tale of Daphne and Apollo (Roman, Phoebus): "Daphne, the daughter of a River God/was first beloved by Phoebus, the great God/of glorious light. 'Twas not a cause of chance/but out of Cupid's vengeful spite that she/was fated to torment the lord of light."

Phoebus mocks Cupid as a mere boy using the bow and arrow that are the preserve of men and gods, but Cupid is confident in his own power and takes his revenge for the god's mockery: "To him, undaunted, Venus' son replied;/'O, Phoebus, thou canst conquer all the world/with thy strong bow and arrows, but with this/small arrow I shall pierce thy vaunting breast.'"

Cupid fires an arrow of desire into the breast of the god, and an arrow inspiring loathing into Daphne's. The god pursues the unwilling nymph, who escapes only when her prayers are answered and she is transformed into a laurel tree.

Ovid's work has influenced many authors, including Milton and Shakespeare. Mythological allusions in the writings of the Renaissance period and modern times are often traceable to the Roman poet.

her love for her husband she felt increasingly sad at the thought of her parents and sister. Finally, she persuaded her reluctant husband to allow her sisters to visit her.

The sisters were consumed with envy when they saw Psyche's palace and its riches. They feigned concern, saying that she might be married to the monster the oracle had predicted, and they eventually persuaded her that she must discover her husband's true shape.

At their prompting, Psyche took to bed with her a knife to kill the monster and an oil lamp. She leaned over her husband to discover his face and found not a monster, but a beautiful, winged young man. As she gazed adoringly at him, a drop of oil fell from the lamp in her trembling hand and awoke him. Without a word, her husband flew away. Psyche tried to follow but fell to the ground. Her husband returned to tell her that he was the god of love, and that although he would not punish her for her lack of trust, he would have to leave her forever. Psyche went to her sisters, who pretended to grieve but secretly hoped to become Cupid's new wife. They jumped from mountains, expecting the west wind to bear them off, but instead they were dashed to pieces on the rocks. Psyche wandered the earth, forlornly searching for Cupid. She met the goddess Ceres (Demeter), who told her that there was no remedy but to beg Venus's forgiveness. At her temple, Venus received her angrily, and set her to various difficult and dangerous trials. Psyche succeeded in completing all the tasks because animals and plants pitied her plight and helped her.

Below: Cupid and Psyche, *painted by English painter John Roddam Spencer Stanhope (1829–1908). The god was originally sent to punish Psyche, but fell in love with the beautiful mortal and eventually wed her.*

The suspicious Venus gave Psyche one final task: she had to descend to hell and bring back in a box some of the beauty that only Ceres' daughter Persephone could bestow. Again Psyche despaired, but again she received unexpected help: the tower from which she intended to throw herself spoke and gave her instructions on how to fulfill the task. There was only one condition—Psyche must not look inside the box.

Persephone gave Psyche the box and she hurried back. Once again, her curiosity got the better of her and she opened the box. However, it did not contain beauty, but sleep. Psyche immediately fell into a deep sleep.

Cupid, meanwhile, had recovered from the wound caused by the hot oil. He longed for Psyche and began looking for her. When he found her sleeping he gathered up the sleep from her eyes and replaced it in the box so that she could give it to Venus.

Above: Venus Blindfolding Cupid *(c. 1565), painted by Venetian artist Titian (c. 1489–1576). Venus is being watched by two nymphs.*

While Psyche hastened toward Venus, Cupid flew up to heaven and begged Jupiter to help him. Jupiter persuaded Venus to forgive Psyche and Cupid. Psyche was brought up to heaven, where she was given a cup of ambrosia to make her immortal. She and Cupid were united in marriage, and in time she bore him a daughter named Pleasure.

Meaning of the myth

Apuleius's account is the only written source for the story of Cupid and Psyche, but it was depicted in earlier wall paintings and other images, which suggests that Apuleius was embellishing a much earlier and possibly widespread myth. In these images Psyche is often shown as a winged girl playing with Cupid. In Greek, *psyche* means both "soul" and "butterfly."

The myth may be an allegory about the struggle of the soul, the reflection of pure beauty, which is chained to the earth by its base passions—in particular, curiosity. Only after undergoing various difficult trials can the soul support the sight of pure beauty. And it is love (as embodied by Cupid) that helps the soul to reach its goal—the divine world of ideas.

Cupid in modern times

Today Cupid is one of the best-known of the ancient mythological figures. He has featured in visual art and in poetry from ancient times to the present.

In painting, from the Renaissance on, Cupid is shown either as a beautiful, winged youth accompanying his mother Venus or firing his mischievous arrows, or as a winged cherub, equally mischievous but more sentimental. In early Renaissance allegorical paintings Cupid is sometimes shown in almost devilish guise as a warning against the temptations of the flesh.

In modern times Cupid has entirely lost any powers suggestive of the sacred or the divine. Instead he is invoked as an aid to sentimental love in popular music, portrayed as a Kewpie doll or greeting card figure, and incorporated into the domain names of Internet dating agencies.

PETER CONNOR

Bibliography

Burr, Elizabeth, trans. *The Chiron Dictionary of Greek and Roman Mythology: Gods and Goddesses, Heroes, Places, and Events of Antiquity.* New York: Chiron Publications, 1994.

Craft, M. Charlotte. *Cupid and Psyche.* New York: William Morrow and Company, 1996.

SEE ALSO: Aphrodite; Daphne; Eros; Jupiter; Psyche; Venus.

CYCLES

For thousands of years, human lives have been governed by natural cycles, such as the 24-hour cycle of day and night, the 28-day cycle of the moon, and the seasons, which in the world's temperate zones change quarterly. Many myths and legends have attempted to provide explanations for these recurrent patterns.

Everything in the universe takes part in, and is influenced by, cycles—series of events that take place in a set and recurring sequence. Some of the cycles of an organism are circumscribed by the period of its existence—the beating of its heart, for example, starts at birth and ends at death. Every heartbeat in the intervening period is a cycle by which the organ pumps blood around the body. Some people think that existence is a one-way journey from birth to death, but others perceive it as cyclical: adults have children, and the new generation begins its journey around the circle of life. The abiding human concern about what happens after death has been the inspiration of countless myths, works of art and literature, and the foundation stone of religions.

The three major cycles that are most noticeable to humans are days, months, and years. A day is the time taken by Earth to turn a complete revolution on its axis. It is 24 hours long. A month is the time taken by the moon to change its aspect (the way it appears to us) from new, to full, and back again to new. This cycle lasts 28 days. A year is the time taken by Earth to complete a revolution around the sun. It is 365 ¼ days long: the extra quarter is accounted for by leap years, in which February has an extra day. Leap years fall every four years except century years whose number is not divisible by 400, such as 1900.

Within each year there are seasons—typically spring, summer, fall, and winter—during which there are significant changes in temperature, the amount of sunlight and rainfall, and the number of floods, storms, and winds. The seasons also govern the breeding habits and migratory patterns of animals and birds, and the growth cycles of trees and other plants, which typically blossom in the spring and wither in the fall.

Day and night

Although a day is inevitably and eternally cyclical, the moment at which it begins is arbitrarily determined. In the West, it starts on the stroke of midnight. In some cultures, however, including those of the Hebrews, Muslims, and Celts, a "new day" begins at sunset. By the time dawn arrives, the day is already many hours old. This starting point for the day is reflected in myths in which everything begins in darkness, and daylight ripens out of the womb of the night. In ancient Egyptian mythology, for example, eight singing frogs and serpents encircle a primal mound that is enshrouded in blackness. The mound, rising out of the dark waters of Nun, shivers and stirs. The Ogdoad, or group of eight, continues chanting as a lotus bearing the sun begins to poke its way out of the earth. The symbolism of this legend has a double meaning—the dawn of each day is both a miniature version of, and a metaphor for, the original creation of the universe.

Among the North American Navajo, color took the place of light and existed long before it. The first underworld was black, the second blue, the third yellow, and the fourth red. The fifth world is where the world as we know it was created, including the sun and the moon. According to Navajo medicine man Hasteen Klah (1867-1937), when the Holy People emerged from the dark, lower worlds, First Man, the leader, built a sweathouse (a primitive sauna) of wood and rocks, and roofed it with four arching rainbows. Draped over the door was a "flashing robe" provided by Grandfather Owl. A "robe of darkness"—or Night—covered the whole structure. Inside, as water was poured over heated, steaming rocks, the Holy People began to chant great mountains into existence, then great rivers, then more mountains. After that came the sun and the moon. The Holy People made a horned sun from

Right: This 15th-century book illustration of Luna (the moon goddess) reflects the idea that time and tide are determined by Earth's satellite.

fire, and wreathed it in rainbows; they gave it Turquoise Man as its spirit. Then they made the moon from ice (some say rock crystal), also horned and wreathed it, and gave it Whiteshell Man as its spirit. That is how the sun and the moon came into being, and it is from them that Navajos henceforth measured day and night.

In an Orphic myth, one of many that derived from a cult surrounding the Greek hero Orpheus, the dark-winged goddess Night laid a silver egg in her sky-cave. Outside, meanwhile, the earth goddess Rhea beat rhythmically on her drum, marking the progress of Night's labor. Finally, from the womb of Darkness, a child emerged, both female and male, with golden wings of light and four heads representing the seasons. That is how light was born.

Counterparts to these creation myths can be found in many other ancient cultures. The details differ from time to time and place to place, but the central idea—that light and life emerged from darkness—is almost universal. Daylight is

Below: Sunset over Istanbul, Turkey. Sunset is seen as the start of the day in many west Asian cultures.

the product of a long and complex process carefully watched over by frogs, serpents, drummers, singers, night owls, and other vigilant denizens of the dark. These stories all have a broader significance, too: they represent the triumph of order over chaos. The desire to impose structure and meaning on the unexplained and the inexplicable is the basis of all human attempts to measure time.

Lunar cycles

Calendars originated from observation of lunar cycles. The earliest calendar is thought to be the 13 markings on a crescent-shaped vessel depicted in the prehistoric cave sculpture known as the Venus of Laussel, which was discovered in 1911 carved into the wall of a limestone rock shelter in the Dordogne region of France. Some commentators have argued convincingly that the markings represent the 13 lunar months of the year. The words *moon* and *month* are derived from a linguistic root having to do with measuring. Other people have pointed out the connection the prehistoric Venus sculpture demonstrates between the lunar cycle and human fertility.

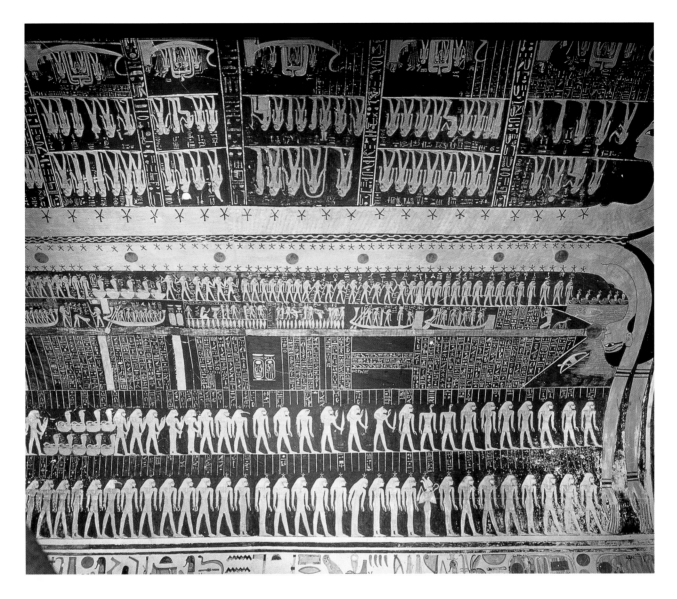

A full moon always marks the Jewish Passover. The Christian Easter is the first Sunday after the first full moon following the spring equinox. Muslims calculate their dates using a calendar based solely on lunar months. That makes their year 10 or 11 days shorter than the solar calendar year, and that is why their religious celebrations slowly progress through the seasons. Thus, the world's three major monotheistic religions base their reckoning of time on an ancient calendar derived from moon worship.

Because the moon cycle is only 28 days long, its effects on tides, emotions, and plant and animal behavior are easy to observe over and over. The moon's endlessly repetitive rhythms of waxing and waning are often taken as a metaphor for human life, which may seem to be extinguished by death but which may nevertheless be relied on to reappear. Moon deities are often associated with magical rites that blur the most widely accepted boundaries between life and death.

Above: This painting in the tomb of Ramses VI depicts the goddess Nut swallowing the sun at night and giving birth to it again in the morning.

The moon is often feminine, but it can also be masculine. Mount Sinai is named for the home of the ancient Hebrew moon-god, Sin. Some scholars have suggested that Sin was a prototype for Yahweh, the masculine god of the Jews, whose laws were handed down from that same mountain. The Hindu moon-god, Soma, is the bestower of the elixir of life, or *soma*; it is said that when the moon wanes, it is because the gods are drinking their fill of Soma's essence. The inner spirit of the Navajos' icy, crystalline, rainbow-wreathed moon is Whiteshell Man. The moon-god of Greenland is so amorous that women who sleep on their backs must rub spit on their stomachs to protect themselves from his advances. In the Andaman Islands (south of Myanmar), some believe that Tomo, the Moon Man, is married to the sun; as he crosses the sky, his tongue hangs out, sometimes a little, sometimes a lot, which explains the phases of the moon. Egypt's ibis-headed moon deity Thoth is a wise god of writing and magic, but he is essentially passive and is only a minor figure in the Egyptian pantheon.

Monthly and yearly cycles

The Chinese calendar is also based on a lunar cycle, its year comprising 12 months of alternately 29 or 30 days with additional short months that tie the calendar to the solar year. Since ancient times, the Chinese have named their months after animals. These names for the months—rat, ox, tiger, hare, dragon, snake, horse, sheep, monkey, fowl, dog, and pig—also denote each year in a 12-year period.

Dividing the year into 12 periods is also a feature of astrology. The zodiac, a combined invention of the ancient Egyptians and Babylonians, is a circle in the sky through which the sun, moon, and planets appear to move. This circle is divided into 12 signs, each corresponding to 30°. The position of a planet in the zodiac was believed to influence events on earth, as well as the life of an individual born at the time. The 12 signs of the zodiac relate to the position in which ancient peoples believed the planets to be at various points in the year. Like the Chinese, the ancient Greeks depicted many of these periods as animals: Aries, for example, is the ram; while Capricorn is the goat.

Seasonal cycles

In considering the concept of seasons, most people in temperate latitudes think in terms of spring, summer, fall, and winter. These four seasons are clearly tied to northern agricultural cycles based on the sun: farmers sow in spring as the sun warms the earth; they husband the plants in summer when the sun is at its hottest; they reap in fall as the days cool; and they survive on stored reserves in winter when it is too dark and cold for most plants to grow.

One of the best-known farming calendars is that of the Celts. It incorporates the solstices and equinoxes as midseasons, and the four celebrations with which each season actually begins: February's Imbolc, the lambing festival that marks the start of spring; Beltane in May, a time of young love and purifying fires at the beginning of summer; August's Lughnasadh, the first harvests at the beginning of autumn; and Samhain—or Halloween—which marks the final harvests and the beginning of winter.

Not all agricultural peoples, however, live in regions where there are four distinct seasons: in the tropics, there

Moon Goddesses

The moon is often female in myths. In classical mythology, the protective Roman goddess Diana and the fierce Artemis of the Greeks are both connected to the crescent moon. Hecate, associated with the dark mysteries of growth and insight, is the moon in its dark phase, a time that prepares the way for the brightness that lies ahead. Medusa and her two Gorgon sisters are associated with the full moon and with its first and last quarters.

In ancient Mesopotamia, Inanna (Ishtar) descends into the underworld in seven stages, corresponding with the seven phases of the moon. At each stage she is stripped of her "jewels"—in other words, her light. Finally, she is killed and hung on a butcher's hook for three days, during which time she encounters her dark self, the queen of the underworld and death, Ereshkigal. However, after each terrible descent, Inanna wins her freedom and returns to the world of light.

Coatlicue was the powerful moon goddess of ancient Mexico. The mother of Quetzalcoatl, the Feathered Serpent, she was honored with flowers in spring as the mother of all living things. Yet she was also the death mother, and her skirts were woven with skulls and serpents. Like many other moon goddesses, Coatlicue inhabits the boundaries between life and death.

Left: An ancient stone effigy of Coatlicue, the moon goddess of the Aztecs of ancient Mexico. Her husband was Mixcoatl, the cloud serpent and god of the chase.

may be three, or sometimes only two. A year with two seasons normally alternates between hot and cold, but may also be wet and dry. The former type of climate is reflected in the Persephone myth of ancient Greece, in which the maiden is confined to Hades during the cold winter months and released to the warmth during the other part of the year. In wet–dry climates, the rainy season is usually a monsoon, but may also be a time of floods, such as those that annually inundate the valley of the Nile River in Egypt. Until the completion in 1971 of the Aswan High Dam, which destroyed this natural cycle, the annual floods began around June 15, increased in August, and peaked in September. Then the water levels fell during the fall, and were at their lowest in May. This cycle created three seasons: *akhet* ("the inundation"), a time when tasks such as pyramid building could be undertaken because high water levels made it easier to ship stone along the swollen river; *peret* ("the growing"), during which crops were planted in October and November, and ripened in March and April; and *shemu* ("the drought"), during which the shortage of water was relieved to some extent by artificial irrigation. Each year the flooding river deposited a new layer of dark mud along the Nile. That fertile sediment aided the growth of a thin, green ribbon of lush crops along the riverbanks. It was with good reason that Egypt was called "the gift of the Nile."

The spirit of the Nile's inundation was Hapi. This deity was connected to the primal waters of Nun, the endless ocean from which the sun had arisen. As creation took up more and more space, Nun was pushed off to the far reaches of the universe, yet continued to project its life-giving energies into Hapi, who existed as a direct link to that ancient expanse of sea.

In art, the spirit of the Nile has both male and female attributes of fertility—the deity is traditionally depicted with both a beard and breasts. The classic hymn to the inundation of the Nile expresses the ancients' gratitude for Hapi's gifts: "Hapi, father of the gods … who nourishes, feeds, and finds provender for the whole of Egypt … abundance being in [your] path, nourishment at [your] fingertips, and whose coming brings joy to every human being.… Thou art the master of the fish and thou art rich in wheat fields."

Most other agricultural peoples also based their calculations of the calendar on the annual behavior of the sun or a major river. By contrast, hunter-gatherers, who followed the cycles of animals and wild plants, had a very different sense of seasonal rhythms. This point may be illustrated by comparing the significance of the months of the year in Western societies with that of the Navajo.

Dates for the hunter-gatherer's diary

The Western calendar today is based on that of the ancient Romans. Two months are named for nonagricultural gods: January for Janus, the Roman deity who guarded doorways to beginnings and endings; and March for Mars, the Roman god of war. Two more months are named for nonagricultural goddesses: May for the Roman goddess Maia, who is often confused with the Greek Maia, the mother of Hermes; and June for the Roman goddess Juno, wife of Jupiter. Two months are named for Roman statesmen: July for Julius Caesar, and August for the Emperor Augustus. February is named for the Roman Februa, a civic purification festival. The other five months are named for numbers dating from the early Roman calendar, in which the year began in March. Thus, *April* probably comes from an old Etruscan word meaning "second"—in other words, the "second month." *September*

When to Hunt; When Not to Hunt

Among ancient peoples, there were many strict rules and prohibitions regulating hunting. In ancient China, for example, animals could be driven to three corners of the horizon, but the fourth corner had to be left as an escape route for those animals whose time had not yet come to die. The Navajo had a similar hunting rule, which was set out in their Mountainway ritual. According to the story, after an elderly father had taught his two sons deer-hunting magic in the American Southwest, he issued a strong warning: "Hunt," he said, "to the east, the west, and the north, but do not pass to the south of our lodge." In this way, the animals' needs were respected and the balance of nature was maintained.

East is where the sun rises, and the Athabascan peoples (Navajos and Apaches) associated this direction with the male deer. West, where the sun sets, was linked by them with night, a communal meal, sleep, and dreams: it was thus conventionally regarded as a female realm. The two points of the compass were joined by the circular and cyclic movement of the sun and the moon across the sky.

According to another legend, the divine Deer-people told the Athabascans only to hunt enough meat in the early winter to last until spring. Then, when they had killed as much as they needed, they were to do the following: If the last deer was male, they should take one of its whiskers and throw it to the east. If the last deer was female, its whisker was to be thrown to the west. Once this ritual had been completed, the season was ended, and there should be no more hunting until the following spring.

Above: The Nile River at Luxor, the site of the ancient city of Thebes. The annual flooding of the river determined the Egyptian seasons.

comes from the Latin *septem*, meaning "seven." *October* comes from *octo*, meaning "eight," *November* from *novem*, meaning "nine," and *December* from *decem*, meaning "ten."

In the Roman calendar, the names of the months show little sign of any connection to older cycles of sowing and reaping, plants and animals. The contrast between these names and the names in the Navajo calendar could scarcely be greater. The Navajo are an Athabascan people who originated as hunter-gatherers in northern regions. They did not reach the American Southwest until around 1500 CE. The Navajo calendar has only two seasons, winter and summer—the change to winter comes in mid-October. Navajo months do not correspond perfectly with our own, and so the following are approximate equivalents: *Zus-entlis*,

meaning "thin, icy sheet," is January; *Atsah-beyazh* ("the month of the young eagle") is February; March is either *Wooz-cheed*, meaning "noise made by eagles," or *Iknee-tsosi* ("little thunder month"); April is *Tahn-chill* ("small growth"); May is *Tahn-tso* ("large growth"); June is *Ayah-zush-chilly*, which means "early greens are grown;" *Ayah-zush-tso* is July, "the month of large growth and young fawns;" August is *Binni-tahn-tsosi*, meaning "corn tassels have come"; September is *Binni-tahn-tso* ("when everything is ripe, and even the mountains are ripe"); October is *Gahnji* ("half winter and half summer"); November is *Niltche-tsosi* ("small wind month"); and December is *Niltche-tsoi* ("big, cold wind month").

Many Navajo months are associated with the stars the hunters used to orient themselves in the arctic wastelands, where there were no landmarks. February is associated with the Milky Way; March with the Great Snake constellation.

Right: One of 12 terra-cotta disks by Italian sculptor Luca Della Robbia (1400–1482) depicting the months of the year. It shows a farmer sowing seeds in the fall.

The evocative names and the richness of these hunter-gatherers' keen awareness of natural cycles hint at a long-lost connection our own ancestors must have once known as well, a sense of being interwoven with the rhythms of the earth, the elements, and the stars.

Modern seasons

Today in the developed world, many town and city dwellers have, to some extent, lost contact with the timeless cycles of nature. To take just one example, there is no longer a limited season for a particular fruit or vegetable, because refrigeration techniques have made such foodstuffs widely available year-round. From this it may be tempting to conclude that modern people's awareness of cycles is marked only by the birthdays of their family and friends and religious holidays, such as Easter and Christmas, Passover and Hanukkah, or Ramadan.

Yet the gap has to some extent been filled by the observation of other events that recur regularly. As might be expected in an urbanized society, most of these come from the worlds of politics, media, sports, and commerce.

In the United States, elections are held every year in November, and the victorious candidates are inaugurated the following January. The start of fall is still noticeable by the change in the color of the leaves of deciduous trees from green to brown, but many feel its impact more strongly through the start of a new school year or the launch of the television networks' fall program schedules. In sports, there is a baseball season, a football season, and a hockey season, for example.

National cycles are further marked by such secular holidays as Independence Day, the birthdays of national heroes, days honoring military victories, and days commemorating the war dead. The start of winter in October is now marked not by a late harvest festival but by the first appearance of Christmas sales displays in the shopping malls. Music also marks the changing seasons: "Jingle Bells" belongs to winter; Handel's *Messiah* is most commonly performed at Easter and has thus become strongly associated with spring; the marches of John Philip Sousa belong to summer.

Yet many people still mark more ancient seasonal change. Farmers, of course, associate springtime with new growth and fall with harvest, while fishing communities associate different times of the year with different catches. For instance, in the Chesapeake Bay area in Virginia and Maryland there are seasons for crabs, oyster, and rockfish. These natural cycles connect people to their ancestors, whose lives were governed by the land, the climate, and the changes that occurred throughout the year.

KATHLEEN JENKS

Bibliography

Ferguson, Diana. *The Magickal Year.* York Beach, ME. Red Wheel, 2002.

Hawke, Elen. *Praise to the Moon: Magic and Myth of the Lunar Cycle.* St. Paul, MN: Llewellyn Publications, 2002.

SEE ALSO: Aztecs; Celts; Egypt; Fertility; Festivals; Inanna; Moon; Native Americans; Rebirth; Rome; Stars; Sun.

CYCLOPES

In Greek mythology the Cyclopes were one-eyed giants generally associated with brute force, simplemindedness, and crude, antisocial, and sometimes even psychopathic behavior. The most famous Cyclops was Polyphemus, whom the Greek hero Odysseus encountered on his journey home after the Trojan War.

In *Theogony*, the Greek poet Hesiod's (fl. c. 800 BCE) account of the origins of the universe, the Cyclopes were three immortal giants who were born to Uranus (Sky) and Gaia (Earth) at an early stage in the creation of the universe.

Gaia, one of the first four beings, created Uranus, followed by a number of elemental figures, such as the seas (Pontus) and the mountains (Ourea). Gaia then mated with Uranus to produce the first generation of gods—the 12 Titans—and the three Cyclopes. They were followed by another group of three giants, the Hundred-Handed Ones (Hecatoncheires). The Cyclopes became the workers, while the Hundred-Handed Ones had a military role and played the part of an army.

In this account of how the first beings were created, the Cyclopes were a separate and significant category of creatures. They came before Zeus, his siblings, and his children—the 12 Olympians—who took over from the Titans and whom the Cyclopes eventually served.

Forgers of thunder and lightning

The Cyclopes were called Arges, Steropes, and Brontes ("Flashing," "Lightener," and "Thunderer"). They were primitive, powerful, and unruly monsters who were twice imprisoned in Tartarus, a dark region far below the earth in Hades. Initially the Cyclopes were imprisoned by their father, Uranus. When Cronus took over power from his father, he released them, but imprisoned them again later.

When Zeus liberated the Cyclopes from Tartarus, he harnessed their power to manufacture the weaponry of his divine regime. They became the forgers of his thunderbolts and they were also said to have made instruments for Zeus's two brothers—the trident for Poseidon and the hat of invisibility for Hades. When the Olympians succeeded to power, the Cyclopes served as assistants to Hephaestus, the metalworker god, in his foundry.

According to some later accounts, the Cyclopes were killed by Apollo. Apollo's son Asclepius, the first doctor, had used his knowledge to raise people from the dead. To punish him for usurping the power of the gods, Zeus

Left: This head of Polyphemus (fourth century BCE) is a fragment from an ancient Greek sculpture. It was found in Smyrna, now Izmir, Turkey.

Above: This Roman mosaic (c. 100–399 CE) depicts the Cyclopes forging a thunderbolt for Zeus, king of the gods. The mosaic was found in the ruins of the baths in Thugga, an ancient Roman city in modern Tunisia.

Polyphemus in Art

From the Renaissance onward, European artists looked back to the works of ancient Greece and Rome for inspiration. Characters drawn from Greek and Roman history and mythology became immensely popular subjects for paintings and sculpture because they enabled artists to depict larger-than-life characters and lush landscapes, bringing out the contrasts and contradictions in their stories.

The Cyclops Polyphemus is one of the characters encountered by Homer's hero Odysseus on his journey home after the Trojan War. Artists used scenes from this myth but felt free to interpret them according to their individual artistic style. Flemish painter Jacob Jordaens (below) used strong contrasts of light and shade to create a dramatic effect, whereas Alessandro Allori's palette of cool colors emphasizes his powerfully drawn figures and focuses attention on the action (see opposite page). Italian artist Pellegrino Tibaldi (see page 356) was a great admirer of his fellow countryman Michelangelo's work, and his version of the myth is dominated by the powerful nude figure of Polyphemus. In complete contrast, Francois Perrier's decorative painting (see page 357) evokes no feelings of horror or drama, but depicts a pastoral scene in a romantic landscape.

Below: Ulysses in the Cave of Polyphemus.

killed him with a thunderbolt. Apollo took revenge on the makers of Zeus's weapon, the Cyclopes. As a punishment, Zeus then forced Apollo to spend a year in servitude to the mortal Admetus.

The Cyclopes were seen as brutes who provided the crude but essential "proletariat" force that drove industry. They were the ancestors of all the forge-working slaves of later European myth who labored for superior masters.

Odysseus and Polyphemus

In Homer's *Odyssey* the Cyclopes are not described as three individuals but as a whole people. However, they shared the same basic characteristics of Hesiod's Cyclopes and were an impossibly unruly group of beings. Their immediate neighbors were the Phaeacians, who were peaceful, inward-looking, and culturally advanced. Although the Cyclopes were related to the Phaeacians, the Phaeacians uprooted and moved away to escape their bullying behavior.

One Cyclops, in particular, has become particularly well-known. The *Odyssey* describes the adventures of Odysseus, (also known as Ulysses), king of Ithaca, on his 10-year journey home from Troy at the end of the Trojan War. His travels through various fantastic realms bring him to a lush region full of potential—ideal for agriculture, pasturing flocks, growing vines, and shipping. The land is inhabited by Cyclopes, giant shepherds who live in small, isolated,

family groups in caves high up in the mountains. They have no form of community or any social institutions, and they rely on the natural bounty of the land to provide for them without cultivation.

Odysseus and his men encounter a Cyclops named Polyphemus, a son of Poseidon, god of the sea. (Poseidon was a frequent procreator of monsters and unruly beings.) Polyphemus was as tall as a mountain peak, completely lawless, and without heed for Zeus or any other gods. Odysseus and his men become trapped inside the Cyclops' cave when Polyphemus returns home and blocks the opening with a gigantic boulder. Their visit becomes a cruel travesty of the Greek code of hospitality, as Polyphemus begins eating his guests instead of offering them food. His guest-gift to Odysseus is the promise of being eaten last.

Like the Cyclops, Odysseus inverts the hospitality code, using it as a weapon against the uncivilized giant. When Polyphemus asks Odysseus his name, the Greek hero declares that it is Nobody (Outis). He then offers Polyphemus a "counter-gift" of wine with the aim of reducing him to a drunken stupor. The Cyclops drinks the wine neat, rather than mixed with water, as was the civilized Greek custom. When he lies unconscious, in a drunken stupor, Odysseus and his remaining men put out his one eye with a wooden stake they have sharpened. The blind Cyclops calls out to his fellow Cyclopes for help, but

Above: This dramatic fresco, The Blinding of Polyphemus, *was painted in 1580 by Alessandro Allori (1535–1607). It depicts the scene in the* Odyssey *where Odysseus and his men blind the Cyclops with a stake.*

when they come to his cave to ask what is wrong, he says that "Nobody is killing me." The other Cyclopes leave, assuming that Polyphemus is deranged. In the morning he has to roll back the boulder to let his sheep out of the cave to graze. Odysseus and his men tie themselves to the underside of rams from the Cyclops' flock and escape.

The story finishes with a moral twist. Odysseus is unable to refrain from boasting as he escapes, and he tells the Cyclops his true name. This enables Polyphemus to appeal to his father Poseidon for revenge. The Cyclops' curse condemns Odysseus to years of wandering and troubles, pursued by the sea god: "May Odysseus either never reach home, or, if he is to return to Ithaca, may he come home late, in bad shape, after losing all his companions, in a foreign ship and to trouble at home." This curse is the primary cause of the long delay in Odysseus's return home.

Links to other mythologies

Scholars and folklorists recognized long ago that the Odysseus-Polyphemus story has parallels with the myths and legends of many other cultures around the world. In all these stories a hero encounters a terrible ogre or monster who traps him in his cave or lair. Often the ogre lives in an idyllic, pastoral setting, which contrasts with his brutishness and primitive way of life. He often possesses treasure that the hero is keen to remove from his cave (gold or silver). Before long, however, the clever hero outsmarts the stupid ogre and manages to escape. Elements of the myth of Odysseus and Polyphemus can be found in the Norse tale of the hero Beowulf and the monster Grendel, the one-eyed monster Tapagoz from Azerbaijani myth, and the northern European fairy story of Jack and the Beanstalk.

Scholars have been unable to uncover the relationship between the ancient Greek Cyclops and the ogres of other cultures or to learn whether the story passed from people to people. In fact, "influence" or "borrowing" may not be responsible for the widespread distribution and popularity of this ogre motif. Instead, it may have its origins in fears and anxieties that are common to all cultures, or to some kind of universal archetype.

Polyphemus and Galatea

Polyphemus continued to be a prominent figure in Greek myth after Homer, although increasing emphasis was placed on his simplemindedness and his pastoral setting. The Homeric Cyclops was romanticized into a country-bumpkin lover, a clumsy simpleton, who was not much of a threat to his visitors and who was pathetically unaware that his aspirations as a wooer were completely unrealistic.

From at least the fourth century BCE onward, Polyphemus was an oafish poet and singer who serenaded a sea nymph named Galatea, the daughter of the sea god Nereus. Despite being a son of another sea god, Poseidon, Polyphemus came to represent a lover who blindly pursued the impossible—a beautiful young woman who came from an element that was the opposite of his own. Polyphemus belonged on land, Galatea in the sea, so his love could never be fulfilled. Galatea, however, was often represented as enjoying teasing her amorous admirer.

The Roman poet Ovid told the story of Polyphemus and Galatea in his *Metamorphoses*. He also introduced, or maybe just gave emphasis to, a third figure in the story, creating a deadly love triangle that turned the tale of an amusingly clumsy wooer and his unrequited love into tragedy. Ovid gave Galatea a lover, a beautiful young man named Acis, who was the son of Faunus and a river nymph named Symaethis. Galatea loved Acis as strongly as she hated Polyphemus. When Polyphemus surprised Galatea in the arms of her lover, he killed Acis by dropping a massive chunk of mountainside on him while Galatea fled into the ocean. Galatea managed to turn Acis into a river, but she had lost him as her lover forever.

Above: Ulysses and the Cyclops: Escape of the Companions from the Island *(c. 1555), painted by Pellegrino Tibaldi (1527–1596). In the painting Polyphemus holds the boulder that had previously blocked the cave.*

Art, music, and literature

As the unrequited lover, Polyphemus became a common character, first of Greco-Roman pastoral (poem or play about rural life) and then of European pastoral in all its forms. Galatea and Polyphemus also became stock figures in Greco-Roman art. The one-eyed simpleton musician was always shown playing and singing to the sea nymph. The pair came to represent a suitable subject for the mosaic floors and painted walls of villas built by the wealthy, who enjoyed expressing their "sophistication" with decorative scenes from the "simple," pastoral world of ordinary, unsophisticated country men and women.

Whereas Homer's Odysseus traveled through imaginary, fantastical lands, later writers and painters often made the island of Sicily, in Italy, the setting of the pastoral world in which Polyphemus lived.

In the fifth century BCE, Athenian playwright Euripides wrote a play called *Cyclops*, which has survived, but the

Above: Acis and Galatea Hide from the Gaze of Polyphemus, *painted by Francois Perrier (c. 1594–1649). The story of the brutish Cyclops and the beautiful young sea nymph demonstrated the dangerous consequences of unrequited love.*

works of other dramatists who wrote comedies on the same topic have been lost. From the 16th century CE onward, dramatists found the foolish love of Polyphemus a good theme for comic theater, combining the absurd, but rather clever, character of Euripides' comic play with the sadly foolish Cyclops, the unrequited lover, of the Greek and Roman pastoral poets.

Composers of opera, again from the 16th century onward, also found the theme of Polyphemus's love particularly appealing. Well-known works include Lully's *Acis et Galatée*, Handel's *Acis and Galatea*, and Haydn's *Aci e Galatea*. There are also numerous works from the 19th and 20th centuries. The 18th century saw a number of ballets on the Acis and Galatea theme. In about 1888 a great French sculptor, Auguste Rodin, created a bronze statue depicting the giant burying his rival Acis under the mountain.

The term *Cyclopean* was used by Greeks to describe the great fortification walls of palaces from the Mycenaean age, such as those at Tiryns and Mycenae. The walls were constructed from enormous, mostly pentagonal to octagonal blocks of stone, which seemed too massive to have been made and moved by human effort. According to legend, such palaces were constructed by the Cyclopes in prehistoric times. Today we still use the term to describe anything massive or gigantic.

ANTHONY BULLOCH

Bibliography
Bulfinch, Thomas. *Bulfinch's Mythology.* New York: Modern Library, 1998.
Hesiod, and M. L. West, trans. *Theogony; Works and Days.* New York: Oxford University Press, 1999.
Homer, and Robert Fagles, trans. *The Odyssey.* New York: Penguin USA, 1999.
Howatson, M.C., and Ian Chilvers. *Concise Oxford Companion to Classical Literature.* New York: Oxford University Press, 1993.

SEE ALSO: Apollo; Asclepius; Galatea; Giants; Hephaestus; Odysseus; Poseidon; Zeus.

DAEDALUS

A native of Athens, Daedalus first found fame as a brilliant inventor. One might have expected the gods to bestow great blessings on such a worthy mortal, yet Daedalus's life was neither happy nor peaceful. He could never resist a challenge, and his downfall came when his attempts to help two desperate women, Pasiphae and Ariadne, invoked the wrath of a powerful king, Minos.

Daedalus's fatal flaw was excessive pride in his work and his personal reputation. He believed that he could find the solution to any practical problem. In many ways this self-confidence was well founded because his inventions were beneficial and admired by gods and mortals. He designed natural poses for statues, where previously their arms had been fixed stiffly to their sides. Such innovations brought him great success, but all the time he feared competition and was sometimes consumed by jealousy, most famously of his nephew Perdix.

Perdix was sent by his mother to learn mechanical arts from Daedalus, her brother. The youth showed aptitude and was a fast learner. As he walked along the seashore, Perdix picked up a fish spine and immediately imitated it by notching a piece of iron; thus he invented the saw. In another legend he devised a drawing compass by riveting together two pieces of iron. Daedalus should have been proud of his promising student, but instead he was envious and suspicious of him. In a mad effort to rid himself of his rival, he pushed Perdix from a high tower in one of Athena's temples. Athena, who loved ingenuity, saw Perdix falling and changed him into a partridge. Partridges (Latin name *Perdix perdix*) build their nests in low hedges and do not fly high.

After killing Perdix, Daedalus fled to Crete, where he was welcomed by King Minos. Trouble soon followed, however, when Daedalus agreed to help Minos's wife, Pasiphae. Minos owned a bull that was due to be sacrificed to Poseidon, but the king did not carry out the sacrifice because he thought the bull was too beautiful to kill. In retribution, Poseidon made Pasiphae fall in love with the animal. She appealed to Daedalus for assistance, and he could not refuse. He built a fake cow, inside which Pasiphae hid. The hollow cow was secretly left in the bull's pen. The bull mated with the fake cow and thus with Pasiphae. Nine months later Pasiphae gave birth to the fierce Minotaur, half human and half bull.

With the birth of the Minotaur, Minos grew outraged by Poseidon's act of vengeance, Pasiphae's behavior, and Daedalus's role in the conception of the Minotaur. The king demanded that Daedalus build a means to contain the horrific monster. Daedalus responded by constructing the Labyrinth. This edifice was an enormous maze with innumerable winding passages and turnings that opened into each other and seemed to have neither a beginning nor an end. According to legend, the Labyrinth was built under the Cretan royal palace at Knossos.

Death of the Minotaur

Minos exacted a yearly tribute from Athens (perhaps because Daedalus was a native of that city) of 14 Athenians (seven youths and seven maidens). These young people were sent to Crete, imprisoned in the Labyrinth, and devoured by the Minotaur. One year Theseus, prince of Athens, volunteered to be one of the sacrifices. Minos's daughter, Ariadne, fell in love with Theseus, and she begged Daedalus to help her save him from being killed by the Minotaur. Daedalus gave her a ball of thread and told her that Theseus should tie one end to the entrance of the Labyrinth and unwind the thread as he moved through the passages. Ariadne passed on the thread and the instructions to Theseus, who did as he was told. When he found the sleeping Minotaur, he killed it, either with his bare fists or with a sword given to him by Ariadne. He then found his way back to the entrance by winding up the thread.

For helping Ariadne, Minos imprisoned both Daedalus and Daedalus's son, Icarus. Some accounts say that they were locked in the Labyrinth, others that they were held in

Right: This fresco from the House of the Vettii, Pompeii, depicts Daedalus presenting Pasiphae with the fake cow she uses to seduce the bull.

Above: The Fall of Icarus *by Carlo Saraceni (c. 1580–1620) is one of many depictions by artists of the moment when Icarus ignored his father's warnings, flew too close to the sun, and plunged to his death.*

a tower. Escape was impossible by land or sea, so Daedalus made two pairs of wings from bird feathers held together with wax: his plan was to fly to safety. Just before Daedalus and Icarus launched themselves into the air, the father warned his son not to fly too close to the sun's heat or the sea's dampness, but to follow him closely on a middle course. However, Icarus, intoxicated with the freedom and power of flight, flew higher and higher. Daedalus cried out and warned him, but the boy paid no attention. Icarus soared too close to the sun and the wax melted; his wings disintegrated, and he plunged to his death in the sea.

Hiding in Sicily

Heartbroken, Daedalus buried Icarus's body on an island and then flew to Sicily, where he was befriended by the king. In Sicily Daedalus built a temple to Apollo and hung up his wings as an offering to the god of light.

Minos—angry, betrayed, and thirsting for revenge—did not know where Daedalus was, but he knew that he could trick the inventor into revealing his whereabouts by appealing to his vanity. He offered a great reward in a worldwide contest to anyone who could pass a thread through an intricate, spiraled seashell. Daedalus, in the name of the Sicilian king, solved the puzzle: He tied a thread to an ant and placed the creature in one end of the convoluted shell. When the ant eventually reemerged at the other end, it was clear that the thread ran through the shell's labyrinthine twists and turns. Hearing of this feat, Minos knew that there was only one man who could have thought of and implemented such a smart solution, so he went straight to Sicily to seize Daedalus. The Sicilian king refused to surrender his friend, however, and in the battle for Daedalus, Minos was killed.

After the story of the death of Minos, Daedalus does not appear in any other Greek myths. Perhaps the loss of Icarus balanced the scales for Perdix's murder, and Daedalus was of no further interest to the gods. His legacy is still with us, though. Labyrinths mirroring his invention are constructed

Modern Labyrinths

Archaeological evidence and ancient writings show that labyrinths date back many thousands of years. Their main practical use was as a defense to baffle invaders and trespassers. Today, labyrinths are designed and built for public exploration and pleasure. Modern constructions of this type are usually made of shrubbery and set in gardens, providing a place where the physical world is fashioned to evoke the spiritual world. Many people who walk labyrinths say the experience is soothing and meditative.

One modern labyrinth is found at St. Mark's Episcopal Church in Antioch, a suburb of Nashville, Tennessee. The maze is an imaginative re-creation of Daedalus's original home for the Minotaur. Nashville has long been associated with ancient Greece, and is often known as "the Athens of the South." Other famous modern labyrinths include those constructed on the grounds of Traquair House in Scotland and the maze at Hampton Court, the former royal palace on the western outskirts of London, England.

Above: Renowned throughout Britain for its intricate design, this giant maze was erected in 1980 on the grounds of Traquair House, a popular tourist attraction in Scotland.

worldwide, and the tragedy of a father's loss—the story of headstrong Icarus—and Daedalus's personality, trials, and inventions continue to provide inspiration for authors and artists of all genres. In the early 20th century, Irish writer James Joyce (1882–1941) adapted the inventor's name as Stephen Dedalus for the hero of his short novel *Portrait of the Artist as a Young Man* (1916) and again as a major character in the novel *Ulysses* (1922).

ALYS CAVINESS

Bibliography

Howatson, M.C., and Ian Chilvers. *Concise Oxford Companion to Classical Literature.* New York: Oxford University Press, 1993.

Joyce, James, and Seamus Deane, ed. *Portrait of the Artist as a Young Man.* New York: Penguin Books, 2003.

Nyenhuis, Jacob E. *Myth and the Creative Process: Michael Ayrton and the Myth of Daedalus.* Detroit, MI: Wayne State University Press, 2003.

SEE ALSO: Ariadne; Crete; Dionysus; Icarus; Minos; Pasiphae; Poseidon; Theseus.

DANAE

Danae was a Greek princess who was imprisoned by her father, Acrisius, to prevent the fulfillment of a prophecy that she would give birth to a son who would kill him. However, because of divine intervention by the god Zeus, who visited Danae in her prison, Acrisius's actions were in vain.

Danae was the daughter of Eurydice and Acrisius, king of Argos, a city of the Peloponnese peninsula in southern Greece. Acrisius tried to kill Danae and her son in order to save himself. The story began when Acrisius was told a terrible prophecy about his young daughter. The Delphic oracle foretold that Danae would give birth to a son who would one day kill his grandfather. In an effort to prevent the omen from coming to pass, Acrisius immediately imprisoned his daughter in an underground chamber made of bronze with only a small aperture for light and air. Later accounts of the legend make Danae's prison a bronze tower. The earliest work in which this version appears is *Odes* by Roman poet Horace (65–8 BCE).

Acrisius barred the doors and left poor Danae, his only child, with her nurse. No man could come in, and she could not go out. While Danae mourned the loss of her freedom, weeping in her lonely bedroom, the beautiful girl suddenly noticed a strange, sunny glow creeping through the window. She was afraid to move. Gradually the glow coalesced into a shower of gold, and then into the form of the god Zeus. He was attracted to the imprisoned girl and determined to be her lover. Danae naturally felt little loyalty to her father at this point and saw no reason why she should not have an affair with this handsome divinity. They spent many happy hours together, and at last Perseus, her son, was born.

Acrisius trembled with fear when he heard that, despite his efforts, Danae had given birth to a son. He refused to believe that Zeus was the father of his grandchild. Still determined to prevent the prophecy from coming true, he locked his daughter and grandson in a wooden chest and threw it into the sea. He hoped that this would be the end of them, but the chest was protected by Zeus. It drifted far out to sea before finally floating close to the island of Seriphos. Dictes, the brother of the local king Polydectes, was fishing in the sea that day and caught the chest in his nets. When he opened it, he was surprised to see a beautiful woman and an infant. Danae and Perseus, still alive, had found a new home.

Left: This painting, Danae and the Brazen Tower, *is by English artist Edward Burne-Jones (1833–1898) of the Pre-Raphaelite movement.*

Above: Danae, *by Italian master Titian (c. 1489–1576), shows Zeus, disguised as a shower of gold, visiting the princess.*

In later years Polydectes fell in love with Danae. Since she had a full-grown son, however, he felt embarrassed to court her. He pretended that he was in love with someone else and planned to be married. All the warriors of the kingdom were to bring him wedding gifts. Perseus, who by this time had grown into a strapping young hero, promised to bring him the head of the Gorgon Medusa, who could turn men to stone with just one look. Surely, Polydectes thought, Medusa would kill Perseus, and he would then be left to court Danae in peace without the jealous attentions of her son.

Perseus visited the Graeae, three blind, toothless witches, who told him where the Gorgon lived. He stole from them a helmet of invisibility, winged sandals, and other magical aids before proceeding on his quest. Perseus tracked down the Gorgon and slew her while she was asleep, taking care not to look at her directly, but only at her image reflected in a shield made of bronze. When he came home with Medusa's hideous, snake-covered head, he found that Polydectes had been harassing his mother, Danae, and that she had taken refuge at the altars of the gods. Furious, he confronted the king, holding up the Gorgon's head. Polydectes took one look at Medusa and turned to stone.

Perseus and Danae were finally free to leave Seriphos and return to Argos.

King Acrisius was still mindful of the oracle but was nevertheless glad to have an heir. He came to love Perseus and found it difficult to imagine him committing murder. However, one day at Larissa, a town on mainland Greece, the young man was hurling the discus at some funeral games held by the local king. Acrisius just happened to be in the way and was killed when the discus struck him in the head. The Delphic prophecy had been fulfilled.

Perseus chose not to take his grandfather's throne, but became king of Tiryns and Mycenae, two great Bronze Age cities. His children included the mighty Heracles, thus making Danae the ancestor of one of the greatest Greek legendary heroes.

Older versions of the myth

This version of the story of Danae was almost certainly not invented by the Greeks, but was based on older legends from previous civilizations. Danae was probably the same

Right: This bronze statue by Italian sculptor Benvenuto Cellini (1500–1571) depicts Danae with her son, Perseus.

early female deity as Danu, who was worshiped in ancient Europe and gave her name to the Don River in Russia and the Danube River in Europe.

The way in which the legend of Danu has been handed down suggests that it was originally a story from a matriarchy, a culture in which women were the heads of the family and in which descent was traced through the female line. Danu was expelled from her traditional lands by invading patriarchal warrior tribes, and she and her followers fled to the edges of the continent. The story reflects the transition from the Stone Age to the Iron and Bronze Ages. Although the children of Danu did not have metal weapons, they were so skilled in magic that they later became known as the fairy folk, or Sidhe.

The Tuatha De Danann, or Children of Danu, were the mythical first inhabitants of Ireland. They were believed to have fled from warlike humans and vanished into earth mounds, from which they could enter the mystical otherworld. Danu's association with magic and the earth links her to Danae. The fact that Danae's prison was made of bronze is a reference to the emergence of metallurgy.

Danae as Diti

Farther back in time, Danae was the goddess Diti, the earth mother of the prehistoric Dravidian civilization of India. In the original story, Indra, head of the warrior pantheon, murdered Diti and her son Vrta with a lightning bolt. Mother and son were both described as serpent-demons, but after their deaths, as a cow and her calf. In both versions the animals they were identified with were the chief companions of the agricultural earth mother. The rivers flowed with Diti's blood, and from this source was born the sun god that shone on the new Brahman elite. This link with the sun reappears in the myth of Danae, who is impregnated by a shower of gold, a metal that symbolizes the sun. However, after the Aryan settlement of India in the third millennium BCE, Diti, like many Dravidian deities, was subsumed by the Vedic gods of the new, dominant culture.

BARBARA GARDNER

Bibliography
Bulfinch, Thomas. *Bulfinch's Mythology.* New York: Modern Library, 1998.
Howatson, M.C., and Ian Chilvers. *Concise Oxford Companion to Classical Literature.* New York: Oxford University Press, 1993.

SEE ALSO: Gorgons; Heracles; Perseus; Zeus.

DAPHNE

Daphne was a nymph who was loved by Apollo. The god pursued her through a forest, but at the moment he was about to catch her, Daphne was transformed into a laurel tree. Today, a crown of laurel leaves is a symbol of success, following a tradition that began in ancient Greece, when victors in sport and music contests were awarded laurel wreaths at games dedicated to Apollo.

The nymph Daphne was the daughter of a river god, either Ladon in Arcadia or Peneius in Thessaly, and according to all accounts she was extremely beautiful. There are two stories that feature Daphne, and in both, Apollo, the god of music, poetry, and light, is madly in love with her. Although Apollo's love for Daphne was unrequited, the ancient Greeks believed that the Olympian god associated himself forever with Daphne by making the laurel tree his own.

Leucippus in disguise

The lesser known of the two myths featuring Daphne was told by the Greek writer and geographer Pausanias (143–176 CE). His version revolves around Leucippus, the son of King Oenomaus of Elis. Leucippus fell in love with Daphne the first moment he saw her in the forest near his

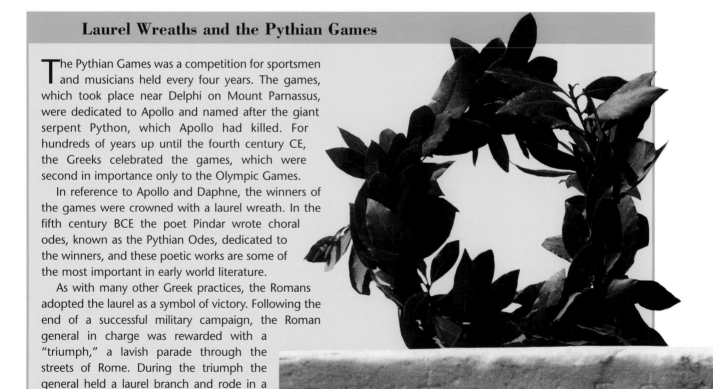

Laurel Wreaths and the Pythian Games

The Pythian Games was a competition for sportsmen and musicians held every four years. The games, which took place near Delphi on Mount Parnassus, were dedicated to Apollo and named after the giant serpent Python, which Apollo had killed. For hundreds of years up until the fourth century CE, the Greeks celebrated the games, which were second in importance only to the Olympic Games.

In reference to Apollo and Daphne, the winners of the games were crowned with a laurel wreath. In the fifth century BCE the poet Pindar wrote choral odes, known as the Pythian Odes, dedicated to the winners, and these poetic works are some of the most important in early world literature.

As with many other Greek practices, the Romans adopted the laurel as a symbol of victory. Following the end of a successful military campaign, the Roman general in charge was rewarded with a "triumph," a lavish parade through the streets of Rome. During the triumph the general held a laurel branch and rode in a chariot covered in laurel leaves.

Right: This ancient Greek plinth is carved in laurel wreaths. Above right rests a replica of the kind of laurel wreath awarded to victors of the Pythian Games.

father's kingdom, but he knew that the nymph had sworn to reject the attentions of all men and remain a virgin. Wanting to be near her even if she would not love him in return, Leucippus disguised himself as a woman and braided his long hair. He then met up with Daphne and told the nymph that he was one of Oenomaus's daughters and that he—or she—wanted to go hunting with Daphne and the other nymphs. Daphne agreed and Leucippus proved an excellent hunter, gaining her respect.

After a short while, however, Apollo, who knew that Leucippus was in disguise, grew jealous and angry. He desired Daphne for himself and did not want the beautiful nymph to fall in love with anyone else. One day, during a hunt, Apollo inspired Daphne and the other nymphs to bathe in the Ladon River. As the nymphs undressed, Leucippus refused to join in. The nymphs playfully ripped off Leucippus's clothes and discovered that he was a man. Outraged, they attacked and killed him with their spears and hunting knives.

Apollo's chase

The more famous myth featuring Daphne was told by Roman poet Ovid (43 BCE–17 CE). When Apollo boasted that he was a better archer than Eros (or Cupid, as the Roman Ovid called him), the god of love secretly shot a sharp golden arrow of love at Apollo. The arrow caused Apollo to fall in love with Daphne. Eros then hit Daphne with an arrow, but this time the arrow was blunt and tipped in lead, making the nymph reject the love of men and desire to remain a virgin.

Apollo tried to woo Daphne, but she ran from the deity of light. The Olympian god chased after her through the forest, both running as fast as the wind until Daphne reached the banks of the Peneius River. Apollo had nearly caught up to her when Daphne prayed to her divine father for help. Immediately the nymph's feet changed to roots, her chest to a tree trunk, her arms to branches, and her long flowing hair to leaves. Daphne had been transformed into a laurel tree (*daphne* in Greek).

According to Ovid, Apollo embraced the new laurel tree, kissing the trunk where Daphne's heart would have been. He spoke to her one last time: "If you cannot be my bride, you can be my tree." From that time forward, the laurel was sacred to Apollo and his worshipers.

Left: Apollo and Daphne, *painted by the Italian artist Giovanni Battista Tiepolo (1696–1770) between 1744 and 1745. The painting shows the moment when Apollo (left) catches up with Daphne and she transforms into a laurel tree. The elder figure near the bottom is Daphne's father, a river god; Eros (Cupid), the god of love, supports the nymph.*

Representations of Daphne and Apollo

Because of the myth of Daphne and Apollo, the god was often depicted wearing a crown of laurel leaves. Apollo's priestesses at Delphi and at other sanctuaries sacred to him wore similar crowns. The Delphic priestesses also burned laurel or bay leaves as part of the rituals in which they revealed the prophecies, or oracles, of Apollo.

The story of Daphne's transformation into a laurel tree has inspired both painting and sculpture from ancient times to the present. Some of the most famous paintings are by 16th- and 17th-century artists, including Nicolas Poussin, Peter Paul Rubens, Giovanni Battista Tiepolo, Jacopo Robusti (Tintoretto), and Veronese (Paolo Caliari). Perhaps the best-known statue of Apollo and Daphne is the piece by Italian sculptor Gian Lorenzo Bernini (1598–1680), which formed one of four groups of sculptures made for the gardens in Rome of Cardinal Scipione Borghese.

Daphne's sanctuary

In Greece a grove of laurel trees stood near Athens. The grove was called the Daphne sanctuary, and it was sacred to Apollo. In 480 BCE, during the Persian Wars, when the armies of King Xerxes I (c. 519–465 BCE) of Persia invaded mainland Greece, Xerxes set up his golden tent at Daphne's sanctuary. The Persian king had chosen the sanctuary partly because of its symbolic importance and partly because the spot gave him an excellent vantage point from which to watch what he expected would be the final sea battle between his large fleet and the remnants of the Greek navy, in the Bay of Salamis. As it happened, the Greek ships under the command of Themistocles (c. 524–460 BCE) encircled and destroyed the Persian fleet in one of the most famous engagements in naval history.

Today a Greek Orthodox Church stands on the site of the Daphne sanctuary. In the central dome of the church is an image of Jesus Christ. The place that was once sacred to Apollo and his love for Daphne is now a site of Christian worship.

KARELISA HARTIGAN

Bibliography

Barber, Antonia. *Apollo and Daphne: Masterpieces of Greek Mythology.* Los Angeles: Paul Getty Museum Publications, 1999.

Bulfinch, Thomas. *Bulfinch's Mythology.* New York: Modern Library, 1998.

Race, William H., ed. *Pindar: Olympian Odes, Pythian Odes.* Cambridge, MA: Harvard University Press, 1997.

SEE ALSO: Apollo; Cupid; Eros; Festivals; Nymphs; Virginity.

DEATH AND THE AFTERLIFE

Every culture, religion, or belief system provides some explanation of what happens—or does not happen—to humans after death. In many cultures, for example, the fate of one's soul or how one would be reborn or reincarnated depended entirely on the kind of moral or courageous life that a person led while alive.

All societies have some set of conventions regulating the disposal of dead bodies and some set of rituals intended to honor or memorialize the dead. As a general rule, most ancient civilizations treated the body of a dead person in one of three ways. The corpse was either buried (inhumed), burned (cremated), or exposed to the elements until the flesh had been removed from the bones by scavenging animals or through natural decay. Sometimes a combination of these methods was used, as when a body was cremated and the ashes placed in an urn or other container, which was then buried, a practice that continues in many parts of the world. In cases where corpses were exposed to

Right: This illustration is based on drawings made during an excavation in the mid-19th century of ancient Celtic graves in Austria. The graves date from the Hallstatt period, around 750 BCE, the earliest known era of Celtic culture. The Hallstatt Celts lived in what are now southern Bavaria and Austria.

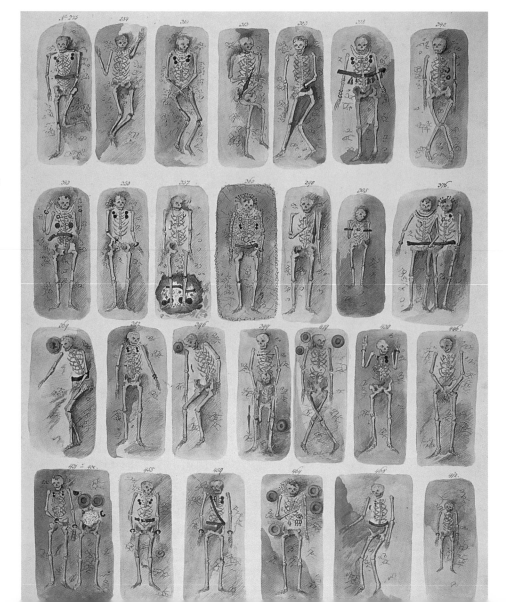

the elements, the bones were often buried once they were cleaned completely of flesh. During inhumations, the body was sometimes placed in a prominent position within a graveyard or tomb for a certain period of time and then removed and placed in a common grave; it may be that in such cases, the person was honored as an ancestor, but as time went by and his relationship to the living became more distant or when the next chief or tribal leader died, the old ancestor was replaced with the new.

Cremation and mummification

Some cultures, ancient and modern, believed that it was important that the body disappear as quickly as possible, usually through cremation or exposure, so that the dead person's soul would be released. Others believed that it was important to preserve the body as long as possible, usually through mummification or embalming, in order to preserve the individual's identity. Often, the dead were placed directly in the ground either extended to full length or curled in a fetal position, and the orientation of the body to the east or west was often important. Sometimes, however, the body was placed in an elaborate tomb that mimicked the design and decor of a house for the living, occasionally even with the bodies of family members, servants, or, in the case of royal burials, the entire court,

Above: An ancient Greek burial site in Mycenae. The stone walls mark the graves, which date from between 1350 and 1250 BCE. Death practices varied from culture to culture: the Greeks buried their dead, while the Anatolians (in present-day Turkey) cremated theirs.

who were ritually murdered to accompany their master in his afterlife (the vast majority of these burials were of males). This practice occurred in ancient Egypt, Mesopotamia, and China.

More typically, the corpse was buried with a few items of personal or symbolic importance, such as a piece of jewelry or weaponry, the tools of the person's trade when he was alive, or objects such as a pair of new shoes or coins to pay the fare for the long journey to the afterlife. Changes in any of these customs in the archaeological record generally coincide with other major shifts in the culture, through either interaction with or conquest by another culture. However, some practices have survived numerous changes in culture and religion. For example, the ancient Greeks provided coins so that the dead person's soul could pay Charon, the ferryman of the dead, for transportation to Hades across the Styx River. The coin practice survived the conversion to Christianity and persisted in parts of Greece into the 20th century.

These rituals only make sense if it is assumed that there is a part of the person, a spirit or soul, that survives the

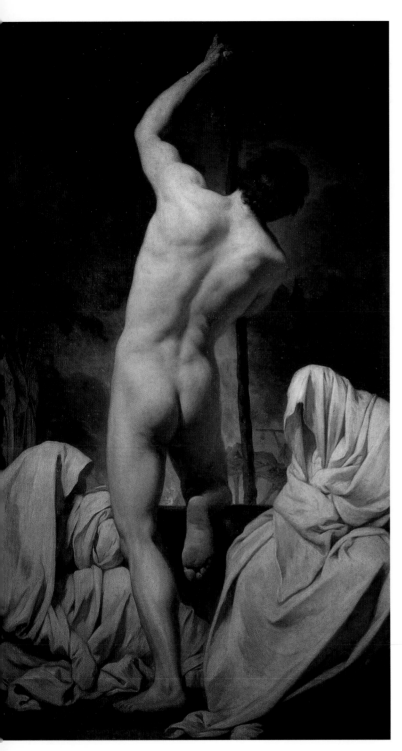

Left: Charon Takes Shadows Across the River *(c. 1740) by French painter Pierre Subleyras (1699–1749). The ancient Greeks believed that the souls of the dead went on a journey to the underworld via the Styx River, across which they were ferried by Charon.*

the gods (often to negotiate on behalf of the community for success in the hunt or for the cure of illness) and, most important, to return.

Often the soul was believed to have several different parts, or else each person had several souls with different powers and functions. In the Haitian voodoo religion, there are two souls: the *gros-bon-ange*, which is the spirit double of the physical human being and embodies his or her personality and individuality; and the *petit-bon-ange*, which represents the conscience. When a *loa*, or spirit, possesses a person, it drives out the *gros-bon-ange* and replaces that "personality" with its own.

In ancient Egypt there was a similar view. However, the Egyptians believed that there were many more parts to the soul. The *khat* was the physical portion that would only survive if the body was mummified. The *ka* was a spirit double of the physical being that could move around of its own volition. The *ba* was often depicted as a human-headed bird that was the messenger and sustainer of the dead person, supplying sustenance for the mummified body. The *khaibit* was a spirit that partook of the funerary offerings but could also move about at will, though it usually preferred to stay close to the *ba*. The *akhu* was the shining, immortal part of the soul consisting of thought, intent, and will. The *sahu* was the incorruptible spiritual body, the part that went to the happy afterlife if it was judged favorably by Osiris. The *sekhem* was a spirit that lived on with the *akhu* in the heavens. The *ab* was the heart, which was weighed for its balance of good and evil at judgment. Finally the *ren*, the person's true, secret name, was the key to his or her continuing free existence. In practical terms, however, the main parts of the soul were the *ba* and the *ka*.

Different perceptions of an afterlife

The idea that the afterlife would be better than life on earth, or even pleasant at all, was a relatively late development, spreading mostly through Christianity and Islam. Even the Greeks, who divided the location of the afterlife into the unpleasant Hades and the delightful elysian fields (see box, page 372), took it for granted that any soul, no matter where it ended up, would prefer to be alive. Mesopotamian myths, some of the earliest to survive, tell variants of the story of the descent of the goddess Inanna through the seven layers of the underworld. When reaching the gate to each level, she

death of the physical body. Some scholars have suggested that the idea of the soul is a generalization derived from the experience of dreaming: the dreaming self is the same "I" as the waking self, but it operates outside the constraints of the physical body, going places and doing things that the sleeper evidently cannot. Shamanism, believed to be one of the earliest forms of religious practice, is based on the shaman's ability to send his or her soul on a journey to the "otherworld" to commune with

Right: This ancient Egyptian was mummified thousands of years ago in order to preserve his body for the afterlife.

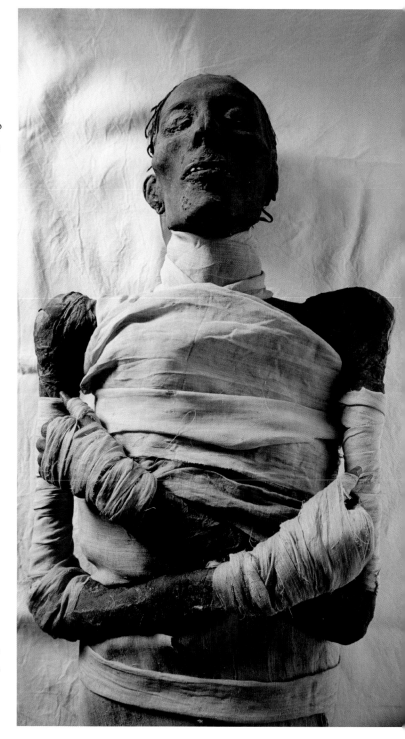

stripped off a layer of jewels and clothes. She finally arrived in the land of the dead ruled by her sister Ereshkigal. Inanna hoped to claim the rule of it herself, but Ereshkigal instead sentenced her to death, and she was hung on a meat hook to rot. However, with Inanna dead, all nature on earth died too, and there was no one to worship the gods. The god Enki persuaded Ereshkigal to allow Inanna to return to life if she could find someone to take her place in the land of the dead. When Inanna returned to earth she saw everyone mourning her except for her lover Dumuzi, whom she found drinking wine and making merry. In anger she announced that he would take her place in the land of the dead, but Dumuzi's sister Geshtinanna, out of love for him, offered to take his place for half the year. This, according to the ancient Mesopotamians, is why the year is divided into the season of life, when crops grow, and the season of death, when everything is barren. It should be noted, however, that Geshtinanna's sacrifice for her brother is regarded as a sign of superhuman love—no one would willingly go to Ereshkigal's realm if they did not have to.

Gilgamesh's quest for immortality

Gilgamesh was a king of Babylon, in modern Iraq, around 2700 BCE. Many myths were associated with him, and these were eventually brought together into one long epic. The beginning of the epic tells how the wildman Enkidu was civilized and became Gilgamesh's best friend and companion. However, as a result of one of their adventures, Enkidu died, but not before describing the afterlife, a place of dust and darkness, where the only things to eat were dirt and stones. Gilgamesh was not only inconsolable at the death of his friend, but panicked at the thought that he, too, would eventually die and go to this horrible House of Dust. He was determined, therefore, to find Utnapishtim, whom the gods had given the gift of immortality.

After much wandering, he found Utnapishtim, who first offered him eternal life if he could remain awake for seven days and seven nights. Gilgamesh fell asleep immediately. Utnapishtim's wife persuaded him to offer Gilgamesh eternal youth, for which the king had to dive to the bottom of the sea and pluck a certain magical plant. He attached stones to his feet to make himself sink quicker to the seabed, where he retrieved the plant. Back on shore, Gilgamesh was suspicious of the plant's efficacy, however, and decided to take it home to his city of Uruk and test it on an old man before he took any himself. On his way he

fell asleep and a snake ate up the plant. This is why snakes are continually "reborn" by shedding their skins. Gilgamesh remained destined to age and die like any other man.

Many ancient cultures believed that the dead were jealous of the living. The most extreme example of this belief was vampires, who, according to one account in folklore, returned to take their loved ones into death with them by stealing their blood, which vampires lacked. Therefore, many funeral rituals were intended to guide the

Elysian Fields

For the ancient Greeks the elysian fields, also known as Elysium, was a place of eternal ease where the most blessed mortals dwelled forever after death. Some scholars believe that the concept of Elysium originated with a pre-Greek, perhaps the Minoan, civilization. Only those who were favored by the gods and had performed many exemplary deeds, heroic or honorable, were eligible. The earliest mention of Elysium was made by the poet Homer (c. 850 BCE), who wrote that it was to be the final destination of King Menelaus, a son-in-law of Zeus. The elysian fields described by Homer were located at the ends of the earth on the edge of the Oceanus River. It was a paradise where the weather was always perfect and no hardship existed. Similarly, others described it as a place without tears, where the sun always shone, meadows were filled with red roses, and the souls played all kinds of sports and music. Hesiod, an eighth-century-BCE Greek writer, claimed that Elysium was on the Islands of the Blessed. Hesiod's Elysium was a place of ease ruled over by Cronus, the father of Zeus and the other Olympians. By the fifth century BCE, writers such as Pindar believed that Elysium was open to anyone who had lived a righteous life, not just the heroic, a concept similar to the Christian view of heaven. However, for the Romans, Elysium was a dark place where souls stayed forever. Virgil (70–19 BCE) wrote that it was a place where the souls of the virtuous dwelled temporarily, waiting to be reborn.

Below: Mercury is depicted as the tallest figure at left in this fragment from a fresco. The messenger of the gods is playing in the elysian fields along with the souls of the blessed.

soul quickly on to the afterlife rather than have them around the living. Ongoing rituals to honor the dead were also meant to appease them, demonstrating that they were still loved so that they would not need to haunt the living.

Death rituals serve to make a sharp distinction between life and death and to keep the inhabitants of each world separate. Ghosts, some believe, are souls that cannot cope with that distinction. They are usually said to be souls that have unfinished business with the living or that are confused about their dead state, often because their funerary rituals were performed improperly or not at all. Thus, many ghosts are souls who never received a proper burial, perhaps because the circumstances of their deaths caused their bodies never to be found. Others may have been buried without the proper equipment, such as payment for the guide who leads souls to the afterlife. Still others have information to impart, such as the location of treasure, or wish to resolve conflicts from life. Some seem to remain out of perversity, to make trouble for the living.

Egyptian afterlife

The ancient Egyptians believed that the fate of a person's soul in the afterlife depended on its passing a series of tests, the most important of which depended on whether it could answer truthfully that it had led a good life. This was usually depicted as a judgment in the tribunal of Osiris, who had

An Early Ghost Story

Roman writer Pliny the Younger (c. 61–113 CE) tells several ghost stories in a letter to his friend Lucius Licinius Sura. One of the scary stories took place in Athens, where a house gained a bad reputation when its inhabitants heard the sounds of clanking chains all night, and often even saw the apparition of a disheveled, emaciated old man wearing shackles around his wrists and ankles. The lack of sleep that these disturbances caused led to illness and even death among those who lived there.

Finally the house was deserted, although it was still advertised as being for rent. One day Athenodorus, a Greek philosopher who tutored the first Roman emperor, Augustus, came to the city and, hearing of the haunting, decided to rent the house himself. When night came, he sat at his desk, writing by lamplight.

Eventually he heard the clanking of chains inside the house, but he still kept working. The clanking grew steadily louder, until finally the noise entered the room where Athenodorus was working. The philosopher turned around and saw the ghost standing in the doorway, beckoning him. Athenodorus merely signaled that he was busy and went back to his work. The ghost came over and started rattling his chains right over Athenodorus's head until the philosopher looked up again. The ghost continued to rattle and beckon, so Athenodorus picked up his lamp and followed it into the courtyard, where it suddenly vanished. He marked the spot and went to bed. In the morning he had the servants dig up the spot, where they discovered the bones of a chained corpse. They gave the body a proper burial and the hauntings promptly ceased.

the apparently contradictory roles of god of fertility and god of the dead and the underworld. He was a god who had died and been cut into separate pieces, then reassembled and reborn; as such, his patronage was necessary for the dead person to be "reborn" into a better life after death. The dead person's heart was weighed against a feather on a balancing scale, and if it were heavier than the feather, the soul was thrown into the jaws of the god Amenti, who had the upper body of a leopard, the hindquarters of a rhinoceros, and the head of a crocodile. Amenti would devour the heavy, sinful soul so that it ceased to exist altogether. The soul of the sinless, however, went to a land of bliss.

Guidebooks for death

The judgment of Osiris was only the culmination of a series of tests. The soul not only had to overcome some obstacles and avoid others, but also had to recite specific spells and words to pass through the various guardians who stood between the worlds of the living and the dead. The many compilations of spells and guidance known as the Book of the Dead were intended to ensure that the dead soul made the transition successfully. However, since the production of such a book required the ability to pay for a scribe to make it, this kind of guidance was only available to the rich. Similarly, it was only the wealthy who could afford to be mummified so that their bodies would be preserved. In fact, originally it was only the king, then the royal family, who would be so honored. Over time there occurred a certain democratization of death, so that an increasing number of people were mummified and buried in tombs, but the tombs were built smaller and there were fewer tombs as monumental as the pyramids.

The notion of a guidebook to the afterlife was not limited to the Egyptians. Another well-known book of the dead is the Tibetan Bardo Thodol. Unlike the Egyptian Book of the Dead, which was intended to help the soul get to a blissful sphere and stay there, the Tibetan book was intended to assist the soul in passing through the illusions of the afterlife experience and either seek rebirth in this world or achieve Nirvana, a permanent state of bliss. To remain in the afterlife was to be trapped. Some perfect, or nearly perfect, souls kept returning nonetheless, in order to provide guidance and good role models for less advanced souls; these were known as *boddhisatvas*.

Various Deities of the Dead from Different Cultures

Akkadian:	Mamita.	**Iranian:**	Yima.
Aztec:	Mictlantecuhtli.	**Irish:**	Donn.
Babylonian:	Allatu.	**Japanese:**	Emma-o.
Buddhist:	Kshitigarbha.	**Norse:**	Hel.
Chinese:	Yeng-Wang-Yeh.	**Roman:**	Pluto.
Egyptian:	Anubis, Osiris.	**Sumerian:**	Ereshkigal, Nergal.
Etruscan:	Voltumna.	**Taoist:**	Zhong Kui.
Germanic:	Hel.	**Vedic:**	Yama.
Greek:	Hades, Dis.	**Voodoo:**	Baron Samedi.
Incan:	Supai.	**Welsh:**	Gwyn ap Nudd.

Above: Le Banquet des Guédés *("Feast of the Guardians") by Haitian artist André Pierre (b. 1915). The painting shows a feast attended by the guédés, including Baron Samedi, standing, second left, who in Voodoo belief guard the place between earth and the afterlife.*

Reincarnation and the rebirth of the soul

The Tibetan idea of reincarnation was adopted along with Buddhism from India. In one way or another, all the ancient religions of India have incorporated the idea of reincarnation, whether it is something reserved for the elite or something so prevalent that even bugs return for life after life. Hinduism and Buddhism teach that souls are repeatedly reborn in a process by which the soul is progressively refined and perfected until it can transcend all desire. Greek philosopher and mathematician Pythagoras

(c. 580–c. 500 BCE) also taught his disciples that souls were reborn. Pythagoras instructed them to follow a strict diet, prohibiting the eating of beans, for example. The diet was supposed to ensure that the soul was pure at the point of death, and thus reincarnated favorably.

Lama reincarnation

Tibetan Buddhists believe not only that souls in general reincarnate, but also that two specific *boddhisatvas* have continuously ruled both the earthly and spiritual life of

Tibetans since 1641. One is the Dalai Lama, the political leader of all Tibetan Buddhists; the other is the spiritual leader, the Panchen Lama. It is believed that the instant one of these two religious leaders dies, his soul enters the body of a child about to be born. However, the infant may be born anywhere, not necessarily in Tibet. Therefore, the lamas' followers must go searching for their leader. When they find a likely candidate, they test him for knowledge of the previous Dalai or Panchen Lama's personal tastes or memories of events from his life. A continuity of personality is assumed to prevail despite successive reincarnations. At the beginning of the 21st century, the Dalai Lama was in his 14th incarnation and the Panchen Lama in his 11th.

Celtic afterlife

The druids, the holy men of the ancient Celts, taught that souls passed from one body to another. However, according to Celtic religion, it was only heroes whose souls were

Below: Anubis, the Egyptian god of death, prepares a mummy for the afterlife in this painting from the 14th century BCE.

reborn. These reincarnations provided a steady supply of new heroes. Classical commentators nonetheless noted that the druids' teachings were similar to those of Pythagoras and the Hindu brahmans. Souls that were not reborn seem to have been believed to go on to a world just like this one, retaining their personalities and even their debts in the afterlife. According to the first-century-CE Roman scholars Pomponius Mela and Valerius Maximus, this belief was so strongly held that the Celts would borrow money in this life and agree to repay it in the next.

One popular form of Irish myth is the voyage tale, in which an individual sets out to sea and encounters a series of islands, each inhabited by beings with a single peculiarity. For example, everyone laughs, or everyone cries; everyone is female, or everyone male; sheep are black on one side of the island and white on the other, and the wool of a sheep that crosses the midpoint changes color. Some historians believe that such myths may have been derived from guidebooks, similar to the Egyptian Book of the Dead, that were intended to help the dead pass a series of tasks and progress to the otherworld.

Above: *The Buddhist concept of the different stages, or levels, of reincarnation is illustrated in this ancient Chinese painting. The cycle of reincarnation is known as a* samsara, *meaning "the running around." Similar concepts of rebirth exist in other cultures and religions.*

Some Myths about the Origin of Death

In many African myths, the supreme god decided that humans should have eternal life and sent an animal messenger to tell them so, but the messenger got the message confused and told humans that they must die; in other versions, the messenger is so slow or distracted that the god loses patience and sends a quicker messenger with the message of death. An Indonesian myth from Celebes tells how the supreme deity would often lower gifts down to humans on a rope. One day he lowered a stone, but the humans refused to take it and asked for something else, so he offered a banana instead. The people took the banana, but then the god explained that if they had accepted the stone, they would have been as immortal as an unchanging rock, but since they chose the banana, their lives would be like a banana tree, which dies when its "children" come to maturity. In both of these explanations, and in many others, the existence of death is the result of trickery, error, or stupidity—humans should have been immortal, but they were cheated. However, some Native Americans, including the Caddo, blame death on the trickster god Coyote, who pointed out to the gods that if humans never died, the earth would be overburdened with people; death is thus the price paid for birth.

Above: A Viking burial site near Ålborg in northern Denmark. The stones around each mound are in the shape of ships—Vikings believed that the dead required this transport for their journey to the afterlife.

The Germanic peoples had definite ideas about the afterlife, and they gave us the word *hell* to name it. They believed the dead spent the afterlife in a cold, prisonlike place. The Norse underworld was ruled by the goddess Hel. According to Snorri Sturluson, the 12th-century author of the "Gylfaginning" (a section of the *Prose Edda*), Hel's hall was called Éljudnir, or "rain-damp," while her plate was called Hunger and her knife was called Starving. A better afterlife was in store for warriors who died in battle. They went to Valhalla, where they fought each other to the death each day and rose again to feast all night on roast pork and mead, served to them by the beautiful Valkyries.

Bliss for the heroes, hardship for the poor

It is probably no coincidence that so many ancient cultures reserved an attractive afterlife for warriors who fell in battle, while the commoner was left with little to look forward to except more pain and suffering. Warriors actively risked their lives every time they fought, and the belief that they would continue to exist and even be rewarded after death helped to reduce their fear of the consequences of battle.

Commoners, however, usually had wretched lives, and the belief that the afterlife would be even worse was a strong incentive to put up with their existence, no matter how bad it may have seemed. It is significant in this regard that Christianity gained much of its early foothold among the poor and oppressed, who found the doctrine of a happy afterlife consoling. Nonetheless, Christianity also had to stress the sinfulness of suicide and the spiritual value of suffering in "this life" in order to forestall its adherents from taking short-cuts—that is, suicide—to heaven. Likewise, the ancient Egyptians stressed that one only reached the lands of bliss in the afterlife if one had led a righteous life in this world. The afterlife always reflected, positively or negatively, the circumstances of mortal life. As the druids are said to have put it, death is but a midpoint in a long life.

LESLIE ELLEN JONES

Bibliography
Pollock, Robert. *The Everything World's Religions Book: Discover the Beliefs, Traditions, and Cultures of Ancient and Modern Religions.* Avon, MA: Adams Media Corporation, 2002.

Walls, Neal H. *Desire, Discord, and Death: Approaches to Ancient Near Eastern Myth.* Boston: American Schools of Oriental Research, 2001.

SEE ALSO: Ancestor Worship; Apocalypse Myths; Book of the Dead; Demeter; Gilgamesh, Epic of; Hades; Hel; Valkyries.

DEITIES

Gods and goddesses are more powerful than humans and either influence or govern human behavior. In ancient religions, such as those of the Greeks and Romans, there were numerous deities; more recently, most of the world's leading faiths have been monotheistic—in other words, they believe there is only one god.

What are gods and goddesses? Some regard deities as real, others as figments of the imagination. Psychological interpretations suggest a wide range of possible origins: A deity may be a creation of the human mind to account for natural phenomena, such as thunder, the seasons of the year, or disasters such as floods; he or she may equally be a parental authority figure on a larger scale. Other commentators have suggested that gods and goddesses are projections of humans' desire to shape their own destiny and to impose structure and meaning on a life that often seems to be random, violent, and short. If gods and goddesses are our own creations, the argument goes, we must be more powerful than them, and able to control them and therefore to govern at least part of our own fate.

No matter whether deities "exist" or not, each of them embodies at least one human response to inner and outer nature. Regardless of whether gods and goddesses created humans or vice versa, when there is contact—real or imagined—between a deity and a person, a creative spark is struck, and a story, or myth, is usually the result.

Cornerstones of culture

Deities, paleoanthropologists believe, seem to have been an inevitable part of any developing human culture. They help society to define itself—as, for example, in legends that describe a god's preference for one tribe over another—and explain its origins through creation myths. They also provide models for behavior within the society—that goes equally for good gods, who are an example, and bad gods, who are an awful warning.

A deity does not exist in a vacuum, but as a focal point of a particular culture. Every self-contained mythology within a culture features stories about the influence of gods on local vegetation, animals, customs, food, weapons, dwellings, furnishings, and landscape. Whatever the local humans use, most assume their gods also require these things. The human body is also represented by deities, and the appearance of these gods is often a reliable reflection of the way the culture sees itself. For example, the large external sexual organs of Paleolithic goddesses suggest that, for early humans, the birth process was the most important human creative function.

Yet in Greek mythology the goddess Athena springs fully formed from the head of Zeus—she has no mother. This implies that, for the classical Greeks, physical birth was less important than creation from the mind. Athena's war helmet and shield also identify her as a representative of a culture that regards the functions of the head and upper body as more important than the sexual and birth functions of the lower parts. Athena was particularly sacred to the people of Athens, and for them the goddess reflected the way they saw themselves—as inhabitants of the most civilized and influential city in Greece. They represented her accordingly in outsized physical form: her statue in the columned great hall of the Parthenon was of gigantic proportions. The form of worship, as well as the images erected to represent a deity, tended to reflect the way the rulers of a society wished to have themselves and their territory regarded by the rest of the world.

Defining a deity

A deity is a being with powers greater than those of ordinary humans, but who interacts with humans, positively or negatively, in ways that carry humans to new levels of consciousness, beyond the grounded preoccupations of ordinary life. The deity may be a creative force that

Right: This detail from a sixth-century-BCE Greek vase depicts the birth of Athena from the head of Zeus under the supervision of Eileithyia, goddess of childbirth.

makes the world either from nothing or from some formless material, such as clay. Some deities had particular responsibilities—thus, for example, there might be a god of fire and a goddess of agriculture. In more highly developed cultures, the deity is almighty, all-knowing, ubiquitous (present everywhere), and immortal—all the things that humans would like to be themselves.

Demigods, ancestors, heroes, and minor divinities such as nymphs and dryads performed some of the same functions as the great deities, but their powers were limited, and their spheres of influence were usually restricted to a particular locale. Nature spirits may have been the oldest deities: they are thought to have first appeared during the Paleolithic hunter-gatherer period, when people roamed the countryside in search of game and seasonal foods. By the streams and in the caves where they drank, ate, and slept, they very likely believed they had encountered protective spirits with whom they wanted to form relationships. From this, it is an easy step to the establishment of a religious system.

Four main theisms

The basic forms of belief in deities can be divided into four main categories: monotheism, animism, pantheism, and polytheism. Monotheism is belief in a single god: the leading modern examples are Judaism, Christianity, and Islam. Monotheism also prevailed for a brief period in ancient Egypt under the radical pharaoh Akhenaton (ruled 1379–1362 BCE), who held that the sun god, Aten, was the supreme and only deity.

Animism can be defined as the belief that spirits inhabit both living beings and the inanimate objects found in nature. The Bon religion, practiced by the ancient Tibetans before they became Buddhists, was a form of animism. The Shinto religion was the nature-spirit cult of the Japanese. Similar beliefs were held by most of the world's prehistoric people.

Pantheism is the belief that God and nature are one and the same, and that everything is therefore sacred—the worm has the same right to life as the great sculptor. Because nothing is venerated more than anything else, pantheism is not so much a religious system, in the conventional meaning of the term, as a philosophy.

Polytheism is belief in many gods and goddesses. The ancient Greeks and Romans were polytheists, and very few of their deities were invariably and reliably all-powerful. Their deities were often fierce rivals, either on their own behalf or as champions of their human worshipers. The epic struggles between the gods became the subject matter of many great myths.

The cave as mother

Theisms—systems of belief that recognize the existence of deities—develop with the cultures of which they form a part. The simplest forms of theism involve the worship of animals. The cave paintings of animals in southwest France and northern Spain, which are between 17,000 and 34,000 years old, are well-known examples of animal magic, in which wild beasts were ritually exalted to godlike status. As the glaciers retreated at the end of the last Ice Age, between about 20,000 and 10,000 years ago, animals and hunters began to settle on lands in Europe that had formerly been uninhabitable. The cave was their sanctuary and came to be regarded as a kind of mother. It is now thought that the statues of humans, which have been found lying facedown on the floors of caves, represented attempts to contact the divine creatress, or earth mother, under the ground.

Right: This powerful figure of an Anatolian mother goddess dates from 6000 BCE. The flattened top of her head represents a crown, a symbol of power.

Interpretations of the Cave of Trois-Frères

One of the earliest images in Europe, in the cave of Trois-Frères, combines several aspects of prehistoric worship: art, hunting, and food gathering. A man in animal disguise follows two beasts that many scholars believe to be combinations of much-hunted animals—reindeer and bison. One turns its head back toward the hunter. Some paleoanthropologists have assumed the scene is "hunting magic," an attempt to snare animals even before the hunt starts. Such scenes are depicted in the depths of Stone Age caverns, perhaps seen as the birth canals of mother Earth. The human in the Trois-Frères cave painting is male, dressed in animal skins and horns, and carries either a hunting bow or a musical instrument. He may be engaging in a ritual dance to assure a successful hunt. However, another, nonreligious suggestion is that the hunter has disguised himself and is merely attempting to sneak up on the animals.

Below: This vibrant image of animals and a disguised man may be showing part of a ritual designed to bring good fortune to the hunt.

Closely related to these cultural practices is the tradition of burying dead bodies in the fetal position. This practice goes back as far as the European Neanderthals, who first emerged about 120,000 years ago. The symbolism of the ritual appears to be that the bodies were buried in the "mother," from whom they would in time come forth again in another form. The practice of burying the dead in caves may have begun as a way of honoring ancestors by preserving their remains in the safest place available. The cult of the dead, with its shrines, red ocher-marked burial places, and honor paid to deified ancestors, marked the earliest development of human religion. From the beginning of human religious practice, the Mother Goddess, who received and resurrected the dead, was associated with the underworld, as were most other feminine deities.

The animal deity was common among hunter-gatherers, whose lives depended on hunting and killing beasts. In the cave of Montespan, in Haute-Garonne, France, archaeologists discovered a statue of the body of a bear cub with a real bear's skull lying on the ground in front of it. This find suggests that the worship of an animal deity involved placing the head of an animal on an artistic representation of its body. It is thought that this was a sort of primitive totem to bring good luck in the hunt. Practices of this kind persist into recorded history: the Ainu of northern Japan worshiped the bears they sacrificed in a ritual that is thought to have been handed down from their pre-Ice Age ancestors. Animal statues with holes representing wounds have also been found in European caves. These suggest that the the real-life physical hunt was seen as parallel to the spiritual hunt: deities and humans coexisted in two overlapping realms, connected by ritual.

Shamanism

The shamans or prehistoric magicians were the priests, psychologists, and healers of the ancient world. Typically, they wore animal skins and horns and took on some of

Above: Villagers in Benin surround a dancing egungun. Egunguns *are spirits, usually the ghosts of ancestors, who are believed to visit earth by possessing living people.*

the power of the animal deity they imitated. Through tribal shamans, early humans were able to placate and petition their nature deities, whether animal or human in form. They were also able to enter into a visionary state, induced by dance and chant: this is still common among Native Americans, some peoples of central Africa, and the Voodoo practitioners of Haiti.

The shaman's state, whether visionary, schizophrenic, or induced by drugs, enabled him or her to enter the underworld, along with the person he or she was healing. When the tribe danced and sang with the shaman, the repetitive rhythms and sounds evoked a trancelike state that made deities come alive in the consciousness of worshipers. Out of such experience, gifted individuals may have gained an intuitive awareness of beings who transcended earthly forms, powers that gave the participants an advantage in hunting and in battle, as well as a glimpse of life beyond death. The shaman's ecstatic dance brought about a merger between individuals and deities.

In a highly developed religious system such as Hinduism in India, what probably began as the worship of four separate elements (earth, air, fire, and water) later became a whole theology with psychological overtones. Indra, the ruler of the gods, represents Being. He is the unified stillness of the infinite and immortal cosmos into which enlightened humans enter. His animal is the bull, and his power is lightning—these symbols almost certainly go back to an earlier animist culture.

Consciousness, or spiritual awareness of one's link to all of reality, is represented by Agni, the god of fire. The early Vedic (Indian) peoples practiced a form of fire ritual that is represented today by the Arathi, a rhythmic movement of a vessel containing flame in front of an image of the deity. Agni's fire is the primal force behind the movement of light and energy effecting all change.

Soma, the god of the mystical nectar of immortality, may date from the period of the shamans, when mind-altering potions induced a state of bliss. In the resulting trance, people felt oneness with all beings. The sun god, Surya, is the deity of divine intelligence and consciousness.

In these four deities—Indra, Agni, Soma, and Surya—can be seen both the relics of nature-spirit worship and the presence of a hidden, mysterious one-god, the great Original, known as Parabrahm, who is absolutely unknowable and who contains everything that is, within itself. It is impossible to say whether worship of nature spirits came first, or the sense that a single divine presence unified all being.

Neolithic gods

Many deities evolved in the Neolithic Age, which began roughly in 10,000 BCE. They were mainly agricultural gods and goddesses who followed cycles, as did the crops and animals of the fields. Instead of being local nature spirits or totem animals, deities became more universal. Their marriage fertilized the fields. The ritual death of the goddess's consort—for example, Tammuz and Attis in West Asia—ensured abundant harvests. The cycles of the moon goddess complemented the rise and fall of the sun god, weaving a tapestry of heavenly events that gave significance and purpose to humans, reassuring them that, for example, when the sun went down it would rise again.

Right: This statue of Indra, ruler of the Hindu gods, dates from between 1300 and 1500 CE.

Priests studied the heavens, and these early astronomers found various deities in the stars, many of whom governed agriculture. As worshipers of patriarchal sky gods gradually subdued earth-goddess worshipers, deities began to dwell in the unchangeable heavens, rather than in caves and fields. From these immortal, omniscient, all-powerful sky gods, so like the great potentates of West Asian monarchies, the monotheistic God of the Jews, Christians, and Muslims may have emerged.

Sky gods and mysteries

From the start of the Sumerian period in about 4000 BCE, the character of deities and the nature of worship began to take on forms that are familiar to modern humans. The earliest recorded civilizations present a pattern of spiritual culture which has not changed for more than five thousand years. The chief deity rules from the sky and has power over the earth. He may demand acknowledgment of his power in the form of sacrifices and obedience to a code of conduct that serves the best interests of society.

Although the sky god made the world and humans, he is often seen as distant from everyday life. The Ashanti in Ghana, for example, believe that the sky god is everywhere and sees everything, but he has no organized cult, whereas lesser and closer gods are worshiped more actively.

Individual religious needs

In general, ancient religions were preoccupied with survival after death, and the nature of the afterlife remains

Human Nature and the Worship of Gods

Humans may be naturally disposed to worship. As social creatures, we are dependent on parents and family for many years, much longer than most other primates. Also unlike other primates, we have a highly developed capacity for symbol-making and language. Uniquely in the animal world, we seek, and find, divinity within ourselves and in other living things, even in the planet Earth itself. We have the ability to see our lives as limited, with birth at one end and death at the other, and to acknowledge deities for both. As far as we know, we are the only species on the planet that attributes divinity to places, forces, natural processes, and the beings that control them—the deities. Yet the modern age is often described as "secular," and many scholars and commentators have written about "the death of god." Nevertheless, the so-called living religions remain strong and in parts of the world are growing in popularity. On the other hand, millions of people live happy, moral, and fulfilled lives without believing in gods or the supernatural.

Above: *The Wrathful Jupiter* *(1810), painted by Jean Baptiste Joseph Wicar (1762–1834), depicts an enraged and powerful father, or sky, god—an image that has remained popular in Christian art.*

Right: This image from the Mexican Codex Magliabecchi *depicts an Aztec priest making a human sacrifice to the sun.*

prominent in modern religions. However, many modern belief systems are now accompanied by an increasing emphasis on the inner self—in other words, a concern with the psychology of the individual. This is not a new concept. While Greece was still polytheistic, there were various intimate or even secret forms of worship that acknowledged a common feeling that some spiritual matters are too personal to be expressed publicly. Perhaps the most famous ceremonies of this type were the Eleusinian Mysteries, which featured reenactments of part of the story of Demeter and her daughter Persephone, the goddesses of, respectively, the harvest and the underworld. It was believed that anyone who participated in these rituals would lose the fear of death.

Among other ancient religious ceremonies of this nature were the Bacchic mysteries, or *orgia*, at which adherents of the Roman god Bacchus or his Greek counterpart, Dionysus, drank wine to attain a frenzied state of freedom from their everyday concerns. Although the details of these rites are sketchy, it is thought that the priests who conducted them also made promises to the congregation—which was composed mainly of women—about what they might expect in the afterlife.

Deities today

It can be argued that the numerous deities of ancient Greece and Rome were replaced by the almighty deity of monotheistic Christianity because of a historical coincidence, but that argument does not hold true in every case where there has been a change in a culture's belief system (see box, page 383). For many people science and rational thought have satisfactorily explained away the need for a belief in the supernatural. Nevertheless, pantheism and polytheism are still followed in some fairly well-developed parts of the world today.

In the West, modern deity-awareness is increasingly individualistic. Many people honor a god or gods privately and inwardly only, and choose not to take part in collective acts of worship in an established religion. Although it is probably true to say that virtually no one still worships ancient gods such as Ceres or Poseidon, more people than ever before have developed their own personal religious codes, which often combine parts of various established dogmas. This is to some extent a product of improvements in international communications, which have given people access to the belief systems of distant cultures.

BARBARA GARDNER

Bibliography

Bowker, John Westerdale. *World Religions.* New York: Dorling Kindersley Publishing, 1997.
Insoll, Timothy, ed. *Archaeology and World Religion.* New York: Routledge, 2001.

SEE ALSO: Animism; Creation Myths; Earth Mother; India; Monotheism; Nature Religions; Paganism; Polytheism; Sky.

DEMETER

Demeter was the goddess of corn and cultivation, and as such one of the most important deities in the Greek pantheon. The central story in Demeter's mythology involves the abduction of her daughter and its implications for the earth's harvests.

In Greek mythology the goddess Demeter was one of the original 12 Olympians and a sister of Zeus. As part of her duties, she ensured that the earth was fruitful and watched over the growth of crops. She also taught Triptolemus of Eleusis the secrets of cultivation so that he could in turn teach the rest of the world how to farm. To honor the goddess, the ancient Greeks performed two different rituals: the Thesmophoria festival, in which only women participated, and the Eleusinian Mysteries, which was a secret ceremony that in part may have reenacted the story of Demeter's search for her daughter Persephone, also known as Kore ("the Girl").

The abduction of Persephone

Most stories about Demeter concern the myth involving her search for and reunion with her favorite daughter, Persephone. One day Persephone, the daughter of Zeus and Demeter, was gathering flowers with her companions in the fields of Sicily, when suddenly the ground near them opened up. Hades, ruler of the underworld and Persephone's uncle, emerged from the gaping hole riding in a golden chariot. He seized the young goddess. Persephone cried out, but only three deities heard her: Helios, the sun god, who always saw everything; Hecate, the mysterious goddess of the dark side of the moon; and Demeter, who rushed to help her daughter but was too late.

Demeter wrapped a black veil over her head, threw a dark cloak over her shoulders, and roamed the earth looking for Persephone. She continued her search for nine days, carrying torches (a symbol of both funerals and mystery rites), until finally she consulted her other daughter, Hecate, who admitted that she too had heard Persephone's cry but did not know who took her. Together the goddesses conferred with Helios. He pointed the finger squarely at Zeus, who, he informed them, had awarded Persephone to Hades.

Left: Art historians believe that this Carthaginian terracotta mask was meant to symbolize the goddess Demeter. The mask dates from the third or second century BCE.

Demeter and Triptolemus

Triptolemus was a mortal from Eleusis who was favored by Demeter and taught other mortals how to cultivate crops, particularly corn. In early versions of the Demeter myth, Triptolemus was merely an honored citizen of Eleusis, but later stories have him either as the eldest or youngest son of King Celeus. As the youngest son his story was the same as that of Demophon, the royal infant Demeter tried to make immortal by burning away his mortality. The goddess taught the adult Triptolemus how to cultivate crops, gave him a supply of corn, and instructed him to travel around the world teaching others how to farm. To aid him in his travels Demeter awarded Triptolemus a chariot drawn by two winged dragons.

Triptolemus featured in several myths following his gifts from Demeter, and in two he had to be rescued by the goddess because he was nearly killed by men jealous of his chariot and knowledge. He also founded the city of Antheia, named in honor of a boy who was killed while trying to drive Triptolemus's dragon-powered chariot.

Below: This vase painting depicts the goddess Demeter (right) giving Triptolemus a vessel of corn. Triptolemus sits on his winged chariot.

Demeter in Eleusis

Zeus's involvement overwhelmed Demeter with anger and grief. She left Mount Olympus and disguised herself as an old woman, wandering aimlessly about the earth in despair over her lost daughter. By chance she strayed near the city of Eleusis, in Attica, which at that time was ruled by the wise King Celeus. Demeter stopped to rest at a popular watering hole called the Maiden's Well, which was shaded by a large olive tree. As the despondent goddess sat by the well, the daughters of the king came upon her. They pitied the old woman and invited her to the royal palace.

At the palace none of the girls was able to brighten Demeter's mood or please her in any way. One of the servants, Iambe (from whose name comes the term *iamb* for a metrical foot in poetry and verse), found a stool for Demeter to sit on. The servant woman tried buffoonery, lewd jokes, and even obscene gestures to lighten the goddess's spirits, but nothing worked. Eventually Iambe gave the sad visitor a special drink, called *kykeon*, made of water, barley, and mint. The drink cheered Demeter, and for the first time since Hades had abducted Persephone, the goddess lifted her head and smiled.

Above: The ancient Greeks believed that winter ended when the goddess Demeter, depicted on the left in this late-19th-century painting by Frederick Leighton (1830–1896), was reunited with her daughter Persephone, shown being carried up from the underworld by Hermes.

Metaneira, the wife of Celeus, believed, like the rest of Eleusis, that Demeter was merely a lonely old woman. Hearing that the visitor's mood had improved, Metaneira offered the goddess employment as nurse to her infant son, Demophon (or Triptolemus; see box, page 387).

Demeter's temple

Demeter appreciated the kindness she had been shown and decided to make Demophon immortal by performing a secret ritual. Every night, when all the people of the palace were asleep, the goddess would take the baby, smear him with ambrosia (the food of the gods), breathe on him with her divine breath, then hold him in the fire of the hearth to burn away his mortal parts.

These secret rites went on for several nights until one night the queen crept into the nursery at the very moment the goddess held the infant in the flames. The queen screamed in horror at the sight, waking everyone in the palace. Demeter, angry at the interruption, resumed her divine form and ordered Metaneira and the people of Eleusis to build her a great shrine in the city. When the temple was completed, Demeter moved in and stayed there for a year, refusing to return to Mount Olympus. During this time the goddess neglected to perform her duties, and as a consequence the earth grew barren. Soon mortals everywhere were starving.

Demeter's reunion with Persephone

Because of Demeter's failure to produce crops, Zeus feared for the existence of humankind. He sent the gods one by one to placate Demeter, but the only thing that would appease her was the return of Persephone. Finally Zeus was forced to relent, and he ordered Hades to set Persephone free. Hades agreed, but before he permitted Persephone to leave, he tricked her into eating a few pomegranate seeds. Since she had eaten in the underworld, Persephone was bound to stay there forever and had to remain Hades' wife.

When Zeus found out about Persephone's permanent tie to the underworld, he proposed a compromise between Demeter and Hades. Since Persephone had eaten only four seeds, Zeus decided that she should stay with Hades in the underworld for four months of the year; the remaining eight months she could live with her mother in the land of the living. These comings and goings of the daughter, along with the reactions of the mother, are reflected in seasonal changes. Winter, when the land is barren, symbolized the four months when Persephone lived with Hades, and the rest of the year, when the crops were cultivated and the seeds grew, she was with Demeter.

Eleusinian Mysteries and Thesmophoria

The story of Demeter and Persephone represented the annual process of birth, growth, death, and rebirth inherent within nature. To commemorate the story and to honor the goddess for bestowing on mortals the wisdom of agriculture, the Greeks practiced the Eleusinian Mysteries. It is thought that the ritual was performed annually for nearly two thousand years, ending in 395 CE when the temple at Eleusis was destroyed. Anyone who spoke Greek and had not committed murder could become an initiate into the sacred mysteries, with the stipulation that he or she never reveal the secrets learned during the ceremony.

These mysteries, historians believe, included the sacrifice of pigs, a procession from Athens to Demeter's temple at Eleusis marked by "iambic" obscenities and verbal abuse, and a ritual within the temple viewed only by initiates. The psychological effect of the celebration was enhanced, it seems, by the drinking of the sacred drink *kykeon*, which may have had other ingredients besides water, barley, and mint, that induced intoxication, hallucinations, and other psychedelic effects. The ritual also appears to have included a dramatic reenactment of the story of the abduction and surrender of Persephone. Chroniclers recorded that initiates emerged from the ceremony filled with joy and hope for a better life after death.

In the Peloponnese the celebration was performed differently. There the Greeks tended to emphasize a darker side to Demeter's character. They believed that Demeter was angry that she had to surrender herself constantly to the fertilizing power of Poseidon, the god of water, and as a result she had to be convinced to set aside her anger. How she was convinced is not known.

Another ceremony, although not secret, was open to women only. The Thesmophoria festival was a five-day agricultural celebration, during which women danced, feasted, and made sacrifices to Demeter. The women believed that they were securing the goddess's blessings, ensuring both their own fertility and that of the community's fields.

KIRK SUMMERS

Bibliography

Agha-Jaffar, Tamara. *Demeter and Persephone: Lessons from a Myth.* Jefferson, NC: McFarland and Company, 2002.

Foley, Helene P. *The Homeric Hymn to Demeter.* Princeton, NJ: Princeton University Press, 1993.

Kerenyi, Karl, and Ralph Manheim, trans. *Eleusis.* Princeton, NJ: Princeton University Press, 1991.

SEE ALSO: Calendar; Death and the Afterlife; Fertility; Festivals; Hades; Mystery Cults; Persephone; Zeus.

DEMIGODS AND HEROES

In Greek mythology, demigods and heroes constitute two distinct if overlapping groups. A demigod has one parent who is a god and one who is a mortal. Heroes are mortals. They may be, but are not necessarily, good: sometimes they achieve their status through deeds rather than their virtues.

Most demigods were the children of male deities and mortal women. Among the notable exceptions to this general rule were Aeneas, whose mother was the goddess Aphrodite and whose father was the mortal Anchises; Achilles, whose parents were the goddess Thetis and the mortal Peleus; and Achilles' adversary Memnon, who was the son of immortal Eos, goddess of the dawn, and a mortal father.

Demigods were not usually immortal, but again there were important exceptions. Dionysus, for instance, was the child of Zeus and the mortal Semele. He became immortal after Zeus struck his pregnant mother with a thunderbolt, then seized the infant from her burning body and sewed him up in his thigh, from where Dionysus had a second, divine, birth. Heracles was the child of Zeus and the mortal Alcmene. After all his labors he was accidentally poisoned by his wife and placed alive on a funeral pyre. Yet the flames did not burn him, and he was taken up to Mount Olympus, where he was given an immortal bride. As a consequence, the Greeks worshiped Heracles in two distinct ways: as a hero for his achievements as a man, and as a god for becoming immortal.

Another famous demigod was Asclepius, son of Apollo and the mortal Coronis. While pregnant, his mother was unfaithful to the god with a mortal. Enraged, Apollo killed her, but he rescued the infant from her body while it burned on a funeral pyre. Asclepius grew up to become a doctor and was eventually struck dead by the thunderbolt of Zeus as a punishment for restoring the dead to life. Nevertheless, Asclepius became a god and was worshiped as such.

Demigods in history

Most demigods belonged to the legendary world of the distant past, but there were exceptions to this rule, too: the philosopher Plato (c. 428–c. 348 BCE), for example, was said by some to be the son of the mortal Perictone and the god Apollo. Similar stories were told of Pythagoras, and later of Alexander the Great and others.

One of the earliest examples of a historic demigod is Euthymus the Locrian. He was a real person, three times an Olympic victor in the 480s BCE. Pausanias, a Greek writer of the second century CE, described a statue to the athlete at Olympia. The statue was rediscovered by German archaeologists in the 19th century CE and found to bear the inscription "Euthymus son of Astykles." Pausanias says, however, that Euthymus was not really the son of his mortal father Astykles but of the river god Caicinus. Various stories were told about Euthymus; for instance, the poet Callimachus wrote about how his statues at Olympia and Locri were struck by lightning on the same day, causing the oracle to give instructions that he be worshiped as a hero in his own lifetime. According to Pausanias, Euthymus did not die but "departed the world in some other manner"— most probably to become a river god.

Another story involving Euthymus is that of the hero of Temesa. Temesa was a small town on the west coast of Italy. Odysseus stopped there on his travels, and one of his sailors raped a maiden, whereupon the locals stoned him to death. Odysseus sailed away, but the sailor haunted the town. The local oracle instructed the people to build a shrine to the hero of Temesa and to sacrifice their fairest maiden annually. According to Callimachus, the young woman would enter the shrine as a living maiden and return the following morning as a dead bride. This custom continued until Euthymus happened to be present on the fateful day. He took pity on the girl, so he hid in the shrine and cast the hero into the sea, thus winning the girl as his own bride. This story blends legend with history—the traditional dates of Odysseus are about 500 years before the actual town of Temesa could possibly have been founded.

Right: The head of the Farnese Hercules (c. 320 BCE) by Roman sculptor Glykon, who copied the statue from an earlier work by the Greek Lysippus. Heracles (or Hercules) was worshiped as both a hero for his exploits on earth and a demigod after he went to live on Mount Olympus.

One meaning of the Greek word *heros* is "ghost," a dead person who continues to be present, though often invisible. The hero of Temesa was a ghost, and a monstrous presence; according to legend, his destructive tendencies could be controlled only by a ritual which was itself monstrous. (The ritual is strictly legendary; the ancient Greeks did not really sacrifice maidens.) The monster was eventually defeated by the demigod and hero Euthymus; slaying monsters is a typical heroic act. On the other hand, even those heroes who slay monsters often have something monstrous about them: Heracles, the greatest of all monster slayers, went mad and killed his own children.

Heroes

When we speak of Greek heroes, it is important to set aside modern notions of a hero as someone who deserves our admiration. Greek heroes were extraordinary, but their conduct was not exemplary. For instance, Pausanias tells the story of Cleomedes of Astypalaea, an athlete turned hero. Cleomedes was a great boxer, but at the Olympic Games he accidentally killed his opponent and was therefore disqualified from the contest. He then went mad: on his return home, he invaded a school and killed all the children. The local people pursued him, but he took refuge in a temple and climbed into a wooden chest, holding the lid down from the inside. Since they could not open the chest, some people went for axes and broke it up—however, they found no one inside it. They therefore consulted the oracle, who told them that they should worship Cleomedes as "the last of the heroes—he is no longer mortal." This worship continued into Pausanias's time, 600 years later.

Heroes' influence after death

The idea of a hero, for the Greeks, had to do not with virtue but primarily with the continued presence, or at least influence, of the dead. Mortals died while gods lived forever, but heroes could do either, and in this way they were intermediate between gods and men. Sometimes the dead person simply lingered as a ghost, haunting the neighborhood; at others, the hero was a legendary figure whose stories were told in great epics. One way the dead survived was in the telling of their stories: to have a memorable tale, or to be any kind of character in one of the unforgettable tales, was itself a form of heroism. All the characters in Homer's *Odyssey*, for example, were called heroes.

Hesiod, an epic poet of the eighth century BCE, wrote of heroes as a separate race of mortals who rose and died out before the arrival of human beings. Some of them, he says, perished around Thebes during a war against the house of Oedipus; others perished at Troy seeking to recover Helen. These are the great heroic stories that were well known to the Greeks and that survive to this day.

Left: The Greek demigod Asclepius with his daughter Hygieia, feeding a snake. This marble relief dates from the fifth century BCE. Like Heracles, Asclepius became immortal after his earthly death. He was worshiped in the Greek world for his powers of healing.

Hero cults

For the Greeks, however, heroes survived not only in fable but also as objects of cult worship. Helen was worshiped in Sparta, as were Menelaus, Agamemnon, Cassandra, and Odysseus, the latter of whose followers erected a shrine in a cave on Ithaca. Hero cults were performed around the grave of the hero and were therefore inherently local—although, of course, more than one place might claim to possess the authentic grave. To complicate matters further, the grave could be moved, and the cult with it. In the early fifth century BCE, Cimon (c. 510–c. 451 BCE), an Athenian statesman, secured his political position by bringing the bones of Theseus to Athens. According to the Greek historian Herodotus (c. 484–c. 425 BCE), Sparta became able to defeat neighboring Tegea by stealing from that city the bones of Orestes. The Greeks believed that a hero's physical remains—and sometimes also his special belongings, such as his spear or shield—had the power to protect those who possessed them.

Above: This third-century-CE Roman mosaic depicts Odysseus's encounter with the Sirens, who attempted to lure him and his men to their doom. Despite being mortal, Odysseus had his own cult of worshipers.

The hero lay in the earth and his power radiated through the soil. Therefore heroes were protectors of the territory. In Sophocles' last play, *Oedipus at Colonus*, the old king Oedipus, now blind, comes to Athens, where he undergoes a heroic death and transfiguration. He is buried in an unmarked grave in Attica, the region of which Athens is a part: because his bones are there, the city and the area are under his protection.

Because heroes were intermediate between mortals and immortal deities, they might (like Catholic saints) seem more approachable than full-fledged deities. They were less likely to be the focus of great public festivals, but people turned to them when in need. The Spartans, for instance, told Herodotus about a baby girl who was so ugly that her nurse took her to the shrine of Helen seeking a blessing. On

Heroines

In addition to heroes, there were numerous Greek heroines—hundreds of them, in fact. Most were drawn from the legendary epic world: Ariadne, for example—who guided Theseus through the labyrinth and helped him to kill the Minotaur—received heroic honors in several places, and there was a local festival in her honor in Crete.

Just as heroes were sometimes worshiped with gods, so heroines could be worshiped at the same time and in the same places as goddesses. In Attica, Iphigeneia was worshiped with her patron, Artemis, at the sanctuary of Brauron. Iphigeneia, according to the local version of the story, offered herself as a sacrifice to Artemis but was rescued by the goddess.

The account of Iphigeneia is one of many Greek myths that feature women who become heroines by the manner of their death. In another myth, a Thracian princess called Phyllis killed herself after she was deserted by her husband, Demophon. Phyllis turned into an almond tree, which, when Demophon eventually returned and kissed it, began to blossom.

There were, however, a variety of ways to become a heroine. Relatives of heroes —for instance, Heracles' mother, Alcmene—could sometimes acquire cult status. In addition, real-life historical figures could be honored as heroines. One example is the fourth-century BCE Kyniska, who was the first woman to win the chariot race at the Olympic Games.

Right: This painting on the interior of a kylix (a shallow, two-handled drinking vessel) shows Helen of Troy, a mortal cult heroine, with King Priam.

the way back from the shrine, walking in the dark, a strange woman approached them and asked to see the baby. When the nurse unwrapped her, the woman touched the child's face with her finger, and departed. The little girl grew up to be the most beautiful woman in Sparta and became a queen.

Heroes were sometimes healers and gave oracles. Their prophecies were not normally on great matters of state, such as the pronouncements of Apollo at Delphi or Claros, but answers to personal questions such as: "Should I take this job?" and "To what gods or heroes should I sacrifice before my journey?" Amphiaraus, one of those who perished fighting around Thebes, had a sanctuary on the very edge of Attica, where he gave oracles and also healed the sick, mostly by sending them dreams when they slept within the sanctuary. The statues of heroes were also sometimes able to work cures.

Above: The fourth-century-BCE Temple of Amphiaraus, in Oropus, Greece. Amphiaraus was a hero who was worshiped as an oracle after his death. People came to his temple to seek interpretation of their dreams.

Worshiping heroes alongside gods

In ancient Greece, it was wholly acceptable for certain heroes to be worshiped in conjunction with the mighty gods of the Olympian pantheon during certain public ceremonies and occasions. The great Panhellenic Games, for example, were held not only in honor of the greatest deities—Zeus, Poseidon, and Apollo—but also in tribute to the particular hero who was buried in the sanctuary that was holding the games. Another example is the Hyakinthia in Sparta, an annual festival that included games and music. The festival lasted three days, and the first day was dedicated to the hero Hyakinthus, who was thought to be buried under the altar of Apollo. Hyakinthus received an offering through a small opening in the altar; Apollo received burned offerings of the usual kind. As was typical in Greek rites, the hero's offering was sent down into the earth, while the offering to the god was sent in the form of smoke up into the sky.

Many rituals dated from prehistory and were formed around legendary heroes. However, a new hero could be created at any time and honored with his own cult. Founders of cities on the Greek colonial frontier were typically buried in the marketplace and given heroic status. For example, in the late fifth century BCE, when Brasidas the Spartan liberated Amphipolis in Thrace and then died defending the city, the people buried him in the market and honored his memory by making him a cult hero as their second founder. The gods were forever, but a hero was a kind of divinity that was still in the process of being created. Perhaps even more important for worshipers, a hero was easier to comprehend.

JAMES M. REDFIELD

Bibliography

Hamilton, Edith. *Mythology: Timeless Tales of Gods and Heroes.* New York: Warner Books, 1999.

Mersey, Daniel. *Legendary Warriors: Folklore's Greatest Heroes in Myth and Reality.* Dulles, VA: Brassey's Inc., 2003.

SEE ALSO: Achilles; Atalanta; Bellerophon; Britomartis; Cadmus; Castor and Pollux; Dionysus; Dragons; Giants; Gorgons; Heracles; Jason; Odysseus; Oedipus; Theseus.

DEUCALION

In Greek mythology, Deucalion and his wife, Pyrrha, were the ancestors of the entire human race. Like many similar figures in the myths of other cultures, they were the only survivors of a flood sent by the gods to wipe out humanity.

Deucalion was the son of Prometheus, and a grandchild of the Titan Iapetus and his niece, the Ocean nymph Clymene. Iapetus and Clymene had four sons: Atlas, Prometheus, Epimetheus, and Menoetios.

Prometheus was a frequent benefactor of human beings. For example, he is credited with introducing fire and pharmaceuticals to them. His son kept up the philanthropic tradition: Deucalion became a kind of re-founder of the human race in Greece. A survivor of an early catastrophe

that wiped out all or most of the early descendants of the first human families, Deucalion became the father from whom nearly all subsequent humans were descended. Deucalion married his cousin Pyrrha, the daughter of his uncle Epimetheus. (In some versions of the story, Pyrrha's mother was the first woman, Pandora.) Thus Deucalion and Pyrrha are functionally equivalent not only to Noah and his wife, but also to Adam and Eve in the Judeo-Christian tradition.

Zeus had become disgusted with mankind after Lycaon, the founding father of Arcadia (a region of the Peloponnese peninsula in southern Greece), sacrificed his own son and served him in a soup at a banquet for the gods. Zeus changed Lycaon into a werewolf, but he still felt vengeful, so he decided to put an end to the whole human race by sending a great flood onto Earth.

When Prometheus heard of Zeus's plans, he informed Deucalion and Pyrrha, and the two of them built an ark in which to try to ride out the flood. The entire Earth was then inundated by a torrential downpour, and all of mankind was drowned, although some cities, including Delphi, Megara, and Lesbos, claimed to have ancestors who escaped the flood by withdrawing to the mountains.

Deucalion and Pyrrha spent nine days afloat in their ark before the waters began to recede. Eventually they came to land on an exposed mountaintop. The place has been identified variously as Delphi, on the slopes of Mount Parnassus, and Dodona, in the far northwest of Greece.

Below: Deucalion and Pyrrha *(c. 1520) by Italian painter Domenico Beccafumi (c. 1486–1551). The painting depicts the pair throwing stones behind them, from which new humans are created.*

Deucalion and Pyrrha gave thanks for their deliverance by sacrificing to Zeus, the god of escape, and then set about finding how to re-create the human race. Zeus, or possibly Themis, advised them to cover their heads and throw "the bones of their mother" behind them. At first the couple wondered what that meant, but then Deucalion realized that it was a reference to the stones lying on the ground around them—the bones of Mother Earth. The stones that Deucalion threw turned into men; those that Pyrrha threw turned into women. Thus the new race of humans was a race of stone, hardy and durable. This story may be based on a pun: the Greek word for "people" is *laos*, the word for "stone" is *laas*.

Thus, ancient Greek accounts of creation place the origin of humankind before the time of Deucalion. The development of the race was then interrupted by the flood, which was sent as a punishment for errant behavior. However, although Deucalion and Pyrrha were not the very first humans, they were the survivors who started humankind over again, and most regions traced their

Below: This engraving from an 18th-century French book shows Deucalion and Pyrrha escaping Zeus's punishment of humanity.

LE DÉLUGE.
The Deluge.
Der Sündfluss.
De Sondvloedt.

Deucalion of Crete

The other Deucalion in Greek myth was a son of king Minos of Crete and his wife, Pasiphae. He had a brother, Catreus, and two sisters, Ariadne and Phaedra. Deucalion became an important ally of Theseus, king of Athens.

Deucalion had a son, Idomeneus, who led the contingent of 100 ships from Crete that took the Greek army to besiege Troy under the leadership of King Agamemnon. According to some accounts, Deucalion also had a daughter whose name, Crete, was adopted by her native island. In other versions, however, Crete was the child of Asterius and Europa, the daughter of the king of Tyre.

Deucalion also had at least one illegitimate son, named Molus, and according to Homer's *Odyssey*, another named Aethon. When Odysseus was disguised as a beggar in his palace, he introduced himself to Penelope as Aethon.

Crete was always regarded with great veneration in ancient Greece, and the Cretan character of Deucalion provides a connection between the island and some of the most important events in the mythical history of the mainland.

ancestry back to Deucalion. In Athens, Deucalion's son Amphictyon was regarded as third in the line of early kings (after the two earth-born kings, Cecrops and Cranaus). The link with Deucalion was so important that Athenians claimed he was buried in their city.

Parents of a nation

The rest of Greece also claimed descent from Deucalion and Pyrrha. One of their sons was Hellen, whose name means "Greek." It is from the root *Hell-*, from which are derived *Hellas*, their name for their country, *Hellenes*, meaning "Greeks," and *Hellenikos*, the adjective "Greek."

Among the children and grandchildren of Hellen and his wife, the nymph Orseis, were the founders of each of the primary subethnic regional groups of Greece. Two of their sons were Aeolus, the first of the Aeolians, and Dorus, the first of the Dorians. Another son, Xuthus, married Creusa and had two sons: Ion, the founder of the Ionians, and Achaeus, the founder of the Achaeans. The terms *Aeolian, Dorian, Ionian,* and *Achaean* are still used today to describe both the geographical and the dialect areas of Greece. They are surpassed in importance only by Athens and the surrounding district of Attica.

Deucalion and Pyrrha were the starting point to which all Greeks traced their origins. As their civilization developed, more and more cities and regions began to claim association with the couple, and that they were central to the story of the flood. The people of Dodona, for example, claimed that their city had been founded by Deucalion after his ark had landed there. The citizens of Kynos, the main port in Locri, maintained that Deucalion and Pyrrha had lived there, and that Pyrrha was buried there.

Meanwhile, the people of Athens responded to provincial rivalry by making new claims of their own. Deucalion was already buried among them; they later asserted that the land surrounding his grave contained a large cleft in the ground that marked the spot at which the floodwaters had first begun to recede. They commemorated this event in an annual ceremony at which they threw honey-wheat cakes into the crack.

The Parian Marble (*Marmor Parium*) is an ancient stone on the island of Paros with inscriptions that record significant events from the time of the earliest kings to the third century BCE. According to its account, Deucalion's flood took place in 1528–1527 BCE, 53 years after Cecrops became the first king of Athens, 110 years before the introduction of agriculture by Demeter, and 320 years before the Trojan War.

Other accounts of a great flood

The motif of a flood that inundates the world and destroys the human race with the exception of a select few is found in the mythology and legends of other cultures, particularly in the Mediterranean and West Asia, but also in other parts of the world. In Mesopotamia, the Sumerian Ziusudra was a pious king who was warned by one of the gods about an impending flood. He saved himself by building a boat while the rest of mankind was destroyed.

In the *Epic of Gilgamesh*, also from Mesopotamia, Utnapishtim survives the flood by building an ark. The major difference between this myth and its Greek equivalent is that the hero becomes immortal. In the Biblical book of Genesis, God decides to destroy the human race because of its wickedness, but warns Noah, who builds an ark and rescues creation by preserving a pair of each species.

Similar stories are found in northern Europe, Africa, Central Asia, China, Southeast Asia, and Australasia. In outline, they are almost always the same: A corrupt and

Below: The Parian Marble is a surviving chronicle of ancient Greece inscribed in marble. The chronicle dates the flood that wiped out all humans but Deucalion and Pyrrha to c. 1528–1527 BCE.

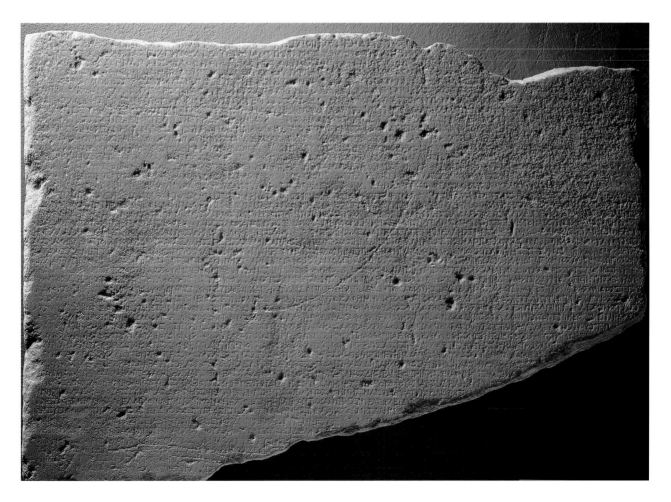

Above: The sanctuary of Athena at Delphi. Many Greeks believed that this was where Deucalion and Pyrrha's ark came to rest after the flood. It was also the site of the most famous oracle in Greece.

sinful human race is destroyed by angry gods in a great flood, but one or more persons are warned, and so he or they take refuge in a vessel to ride out the waters of the flood. The survivors then become the ancestors through whom humankind, and often other species as well, are able to continue. An occasional variant on this basic theme is that the gods send the flood because Earth was becoming overpopulated by humans.

Historical basis

Recent geological discoveries have led archaeologists and other scholars to propose that what is now the Black Sea was once an enclosed freshwater lake. In about 7000 BCE, however, it burst its banks at what is now the Bosporus and Dardanelles, and opened out into the Mediterranean Sea, causing extensive flooding in the eastern Mediterranean and beyond. If that is correct, the Greek and West Asian myths of a great flood may be a "folk memory" of this cataclysmic event.

Although the breach of the ancient topographical barrier between the Black Sea and the Mediterranean Sea is an event of immense significance, the flood myths retain a broader and perhaps even greater symbolic importance. The stories can be viewed as a metaphor for one of the most fundamental preoccupations of human experience: the fear of being engulfed and swept away in a huge, elemental catastrophe. Whether such a worldwide disaster ever actually took place is thus, to some extent, a relatively minor consideration.

Deucalion is featured very little in what remains of ancient Greek art, but the theme of the great flood became popular during the Renaissance in Europe, and various Italian painters depicted topics such as the flood involving Deucalion and Pyrrha. The leading works on these themes are by Baldassare Peruzzi (1481–1536), Lo Schiavone (1522–1563), Lelio Orsi (c. 1511–1587), and Giovanni Castiglione (c. 1616–1670). The topic was also favored for a while in minor operatic works by composers of the late 18th and early 19th centuries.

ANTHONY BULLOCH

Bibliography

Bulfinch, Thomas. *Myths of Greece and Rome.* New York: Viking Penguin, Inc., 1998.

Howatson, M.C., and Ian Chilvers. *Concise Oxford Companion to Classical Literature.* New York: Oxford University Press, 1993.

SEE ALSO: Apocalypse Myths; Crete; Flood Myths; Odysseus; Pandora; Prometheus; Zeus.

DEVILS

In many cultures around the world devils, demons, and evil spirits represented in one way or another all that humans considered bad, from moral weakness to natural disasters. The concept of devils and evil also served a useful purpose, particularly in insular cultures, by teaching children to avoid dangers and to behave in ways appropriate to the social and moral codes of the group.

Generally, in the Abrahamic religions—Judaism, Christianity, and Islam—the devil is the mythic ruler of evil. Evil is an abstract concept that refers to each subculture's understanding of morally reprehensible or wicked acts. The biblical devil is also the rival of the more powerful, omnipotent creator deity, God. In many other non-Abrahamic cultures around the world, devils, demons, evil spirits, and even cruel acts performed by the gods were useful for explaining the causes of those fearful things that our ancestors did not understand, whether in terms of human behavior, such as sexual desire; birth defects and other physiological abnormalities; mental illness; or natural occurrences, including earthquakes, hurricanes, and droughts.

Many ancient polytheistic cultures did not have devils or demons but instead blamed the gods for misfortune and ill occurrences. Most deities had moments when they behaved badly, irrationally, or selfishly, either causing humans to do evil things or making natural disasters occur. Also, unlike the orthodox Christian view of hell being ruled by Satan, for most polytheistic belief systems, the ruler of the underworld was not the personification of evil. For example, the Greek Hades behaved no more selfishly or cruelly than any other Olympian, and his queen, Persephone, was responsible in part for ensuring good

Above: The devil on this French tarot card has bird's claws, a serpent's tail, and wings. Depictions of the devil vary around the world.

harvests. Another example is the Etruscan goddess of death, Vanth. She accompanied Charu, who was a kind of grim reaper, when he appeared near the moment of death to take the dying person's soul to the underworld. Vanth's role was to comfort the dying person and ease his or her transition to death.

Left: This copy of a Persian frieze from the fifth century BCE depicts the good deity, Ahura Mazda, defeating the evil deity, Angra Mainyu.

drugs, and one of the leading *drugs* was Agas (Evil Eye), the demon of illness. Together the *devas* and *drugs* fought Ahuru Mazda and his good-spirit servants, the *amesha spentas*. Persians believed that in a final battle of judgment, human souls would endure a fiery ordeal and only the good would survive. In that way Zoroastrianism urged its followers to live their lives in the way of the god of light and to shun the evil god of darkness.

In the Old Testament the appearance of the devil occurs only occasionally, in Genesis, Job, Kings, and elsewhere, but in the Talmud and other rabbinical works the devil is far more prevalent; it exists too in Jewish folklore. Some rabbinical teachings claim that demons are in the air and that humans are constantly under threat of allowing them into their systems. This same idea of the ubiquity of evil was inherited by Christianity.

Demons in polytheistic cultures

In many parts of the world, such as Africa, the Americas, Asia, and Oceania, spirits were thought to exist in and as part of the natural world, and in most cases the spirits, like humans or Greek deities, were neither wholly good nor wholly bad. However, there are exceptions, such as Mara, the evil demon of Buddhist mythology. Mara is the master magician of illusion, the manifestation of evil, and the tempter of the divine Gautama. A demonic creature, Mara is usually depicted as having a hundred arms and riding an elephant. The demon attacked the original Buddha, Gautama, as the deity-priest sat in meditation under a banyan tree, but Gautama gathered the gods to him for strength, and Mara vanished. Contemporary Buddhists believe that Mara waits to seize dying souls at the edge of the world.

Many demons or evil gods in polytheistic belief systems may well have originally been good deities. When one polytheistic culture dominated another, they would usually merge the pantheon of both, but alter the defeated culture's deities by making some of them either less powerful or even totally evil. For example, scholars believe that in ancient Egypt, Seth was an important deity of a Semitic culture called the Hyksos, who temporarily occupied Upper Egypt in the 17th century BCE. When the Hyksos were removed from power, the Egyptians turned Seth into an evil god who battled the savior deity Osiris.

A more complex character is Kali (Black One), the Hindu mother goddess, a symbol of dissolution and

Devils in monotheistic religions

The word *devil* comes from the Greek *diabolos,* meaning "adversary," "prosecutor," and "to slander." The Greek word is derived from the Indo-European root word for *deva,* meaning "angel," and in Christian belief the devil is a fallen angel. There are numerous nicknames for the the devil, such as Satan, Beelzebub, Mephistopheles, Lucifer, Prince of Darkness, and Old Scratch. The Judeo-Christian concept of embodying evil in a single figure can be traced back to Zoroastrianism, an ancient Persian religion. Zoroastrian theology was based on two gods, one good and one evil, who waged a cosmic struggle. Ahura Mazda, or Ormazd (Wise Lord), was the god of light, and Ahriman, or Angra Mainyu (Evil Spirit) was the god of darkness. *Devas* were the male demon spirits that served Angra Mainyu, causing plagues and diseases. Female demon spirits were called

Left: This sculptured relief from the fourth or third century BCE is of Vanth, the Etruscan goddess of death, who comforted the dying.

destruction, and the grim consort of Siva, the chief deity of destruction. Originally, Kali destroyed ignorance, maintained world order, and blessed those searching for spiritual knowledge, so historically she may have belonged to an ancient, vanquished culture in India. Then at some point the name Kali became associated with Agni, the god of fire who had seven flickering tongues of flame; Kali was also the name given to his black, horrible tongue. Kali the goddess became a fearsome being with baleful eyes, protruding tongue, and four arms. In most depictions she wields a bloodied sword in her upper left hand, holds the severed head of a demon in her lower left hand, makes a gesture of fearlessness with her upper right hand, and confers benefits on worshipers with her lower right hand. A chain of severed human heads drapes around her, and her belt is made of dismembered human arms. Worshipers of Kali live primarily in Bengal, and her best-known temples are in Kalighat and Dakshineshvara.

Catalyst for creation

In some cases the destruction of evil creatures or deities led to the creation of the world. In ancient Babylonian mythology, Tiamat was a bloated female dragon that personified the saltwater ocean of Chaos, the primordial mother of everything and all the gods. In the creation myth *Enuma Elish,* from around 1900 BCE, Tiamat and her consort Apsu determined to kill their offspring. One of them, Ea, managed to murder Apsu first, and Tiamat flew into a rage. She created an army of vengeful monstrous creatures, led by her new consort, Kingu (also her son). The young god Marduk, who was born in the deep freshwater sea, defeated Tiamat by cleaving her body in two. Marduk then made the earth from the lower half of Tiamat's severed body and the sky from the upper half. The clouds came from Tiamat's bodily fluids, and the dragon's tears were the source of the Tigris and Euphrates rivers. Tiamat, therefore, is both a dangerous goddess and the source of creation. In an ancient myth from Siberia, Ulgan, the creator, commanded the first man to bring a piece of soil from the primeval ocean. Ulgan planned to make the world by throwing the earth into the primordial water. Wanting to create a world of his own, Erlik, the spirit of evil, hid a piece of the same earth in his mouth, but the soil expanded, choking the demon deity. Ulgan commanded Erlik to spit out the soil, which became marshlands.

One important North American mythic character is the Coyote, a trickster deity popular among indigenous peoples of California, the Southwest, and Plateau regions. Coyote desires to make human life more interesting, partly by causing the creation of sickness, sorrow, and death. Any destructive natural phenomena, as well as beneficial inventions, are recognized as the result of Coyote's creative but mischievous power. The trickster figure is also common among Indian groups in other parts of North America, as

Right: The demon of evil, Mara, is depicted surrounding the center of this Buddhist illustration of the Wheel of Life. Mara stands outside the wheel to try to capture the souls of those who have just died. She was vanquished by Gautama, the first Buddha.

well as in South America, Africa, Japan, and Oceania. Depending on the mythology, the trickster appears variously as a hare, spider, or fox, among other forms, and can be both creator and destroyer, innocent fool and conniving deceiver. Sometimes the trickster's pranks are harmless and evoke humor. At other times they can be extremely dangerous. Scholars believe that tricksters, like the demons and devils of some cultures, symbolize the collective fears and failures of the source culture.

Purely evil devils

Some polytheistic belief systems feature minor gods intent on performing only evil and destruction. In ancient Sumer, demons inhabited fire, plagues, and other diseases, natural disasters such as droughts, and sudden infant death syndrome. The most infamous Sumerian demon was the Pazuzu, which was depicted as having four wings, clawed feet, and a lion's head or face. Ancient demons, like Pazuzu, were often made up of a combination of two or more animals, such as scorpions, serpents, goats, and eagles. Combating such evil creatures involved performing sacred rituals, incantations, and the use of charms. Such practices continue today in many parts of the world, notably in the Caribbean, where some people practice voodoo.

Scottish Devils

In Scottish folklore Kelpie was a treacherous water devil who lurked in lakes and rivers, usually assuming the shape of a young horse. It was said that if a tired traveler stopped by a lake to rest or have a drink and saw a horse grazing peacefully, the traveler must never mount the horse for fear that it was really Kelpie. If the traveler did mount Kelpie, the demon would dive into the water and drown the traveler.

In Scotland another name for the devil is Black Donald, and he excels at all jobs except tailoring because tailors never taught him the baste stitch. Black Donald has many disguises, including an old man in a black suit, but he always gives himself away because of his cloven feet. The devil is also called Auld or Old Clootie (Auld or Old Cloots), derived from *cloot*, the word for one division of a cleft hoof. Scottish farmers traditionally leave a small piece of their land untilled as a gift to the devil: they call it Clootie's Croft.

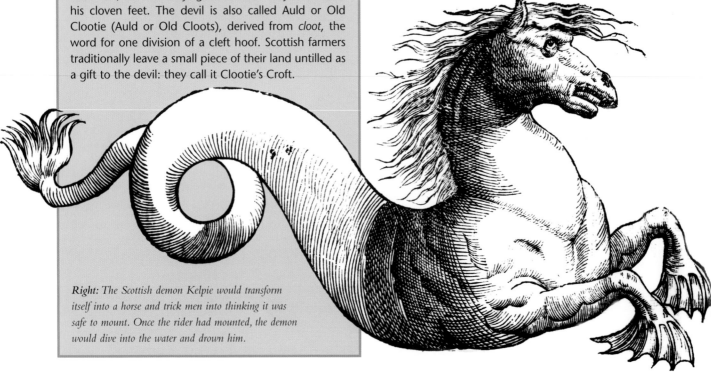

Right: The Scottish demon Kelpie would transform itself into a horse and trick men into thinking it was safe to mount. Once the rider had mounted, the demon would dive into the water and drown him.

Japanese *Oni*

The *oni* are demons of Japanese Buddhism. They are depicted as being similar to humans, except that they usually have three eyes, big mouths, horns, and sharp nails. They also fly around and seize wicked souls on their deathbeds. The spirit of Shoki is the main thing that the demons fear. Shoki was a physician during the T'ang Dynasty (618–907 CE) whose spirit vowed to protect the Japanese against evil. Today statues of Shoki are placed outside homes, especially where young children live, to ward off the *oni*.

The *oni* also play a part in what happens to the souls of miscarried babies. These souls are supposed to go to heaven and get close to the gods. Burdened by carrying their parents' guilt, the dead babies' souls cannot cross the Milky Way, but are stuck having nothing to do but play, making mountains with rocks. The *oni* come and destroy the mountains, scaring the baby souls by surrounding them with darkness. The babies cry and call for their mothers in vain, putting their rock mountains back together in the dark. Knowing this sad story, Japanese women help the baby souls find their way to heaven by praying for light and guidance. Such prayers by women occur most often at the Haruna Temple, built 400 years ago for women who had miscarried.

Another Japanese demon is Raiju ("Thunder Animal"), a demon of lightning in the shape of a cat, badger, or weasel. During thunderstorms, Raiju becomes agitated and leaps from tree to tree, clawing trees struck by lightning. At other times Raiju likes to hide in human navels; the Japanese believe that sleeping on one's stomach protects them from Raiju.

Left: This wooden carving of an oni *dates to the late 18th century.* Oni *are believed to have the ability to seize peoples' souls.*

Some devils specifically target women. For example, in Japanese mythology, Kitsune-Tsuki was a demon spirit who took the form of a fox and could also possess women by entering their bodies through their fingernails or breasts. Similarly, the mejenkwaar were female demons in the Marshall Islands who tried to possess pregnant women while their husbands were away collecting special gifts. If the husband was gone for too long, it was possible that the pregnant woman would be turned into a mejenkwaad by the mejenkwaar and eat or otherwise kill her newborn child. The mejenkwaad would also attack her husband when he returned. Perhaps the mejenkwaad provided an explanation for the natural condition known as postpartum depression. One myth explains that a husband was able to avoid being eaten by his wife-turned-mejenkwaad by outwitting her with several tricks.

Native American mythology includes many devils, such as Wan-nioni, a dust devil of the peoples of the Great Plains, youngest brother to the Four winds. In Iroquois mythology, Malsum, god of darkness, created monsters and plagues that would torment humans. He made plants have spines, insects have stings, and animals have teeth and claws. In Ojibwa mythology, the Windigo were devil-like cannibalistic monsters living in forests and preying on humans. The Hurons believed in Tawiskara, the evil twin of the good deity Ioskeha. The brothers dueled for control of the world, each taking up whatever he could find as a weapon. Tawiskara fought with a rose-twig and was defeated by Ioskeha, who used a stag's antlers. Tawiskara fled into exile, weeping flint tears.

ALYS CAVINESS

Bibliography

Cotterell, Arthur. *Oxford Dictionary of World Mythology*. New York: Oxford University Press, 1997.

Forsyth, Neil. *The Old Enemy*. Princeton, NJ: Princeton University Press, 1989.

Pagels, Elaine. *The Origin of Satan*. New York: Vintage Books, 1996.

SEE ALSO: Animal-headed Figures; Apocalypse Myths; Death and the Afterlife; Hades; Hel.

DIANA

Diana was originally an ancient Italian goddess of the hunt, but the Romans later attributed to her many of the myths and characteristics of the Greek goddess Artemis. A cult dedicated to Diana was centered on a grove at Aricia, near Lake Nemi, between Rome and Naples.

Many Indo-European cultures had a goddess of the hunt. The Greek version was Artemis, and her main characteristics and the greatest of her powers were taken up by the Romans and ascribed to their own deity, Diana. However, Diana also had some unique traits of her own.

The name Diana probably means "bright one." The first syllable (*di-*) may come from an Indo-European word meaning "to shine."

Diana was closely identified with the moon, which she personified in all its phases—waxing, full, and waning. Because the human female cycle of ovulation, like the phases of the moon, occupies a 28-day period, Diana also became the goddess of women in pregnancy and childbirth. She was responsible for young maidens' success in marriage, but not for love and sex, which were ruled by Venus.

Diana was, in addition, the protectress of wild animals—this did not conflict with her responsibilities for the hunt, because she looked after young and pregnant creatures, neither of which are hunted as game.

Divine trinity

Diana is described both as a wife and as a daughter of Jupiter (Zeus). She became closely associated with two other deities, and together they formed a trinity. One was the water nymph Egeria, who became Diana's

Right: This sculpture of Diana shows the goddess within both her temple (above her head) and an oak tree (below her waist).

servant and assistant midwife after the death of Egeria's lover, Numa Pompilius, the second king of Rome. According to legend, Egeria cried so much at his loss that Diana turned her into an eternal spring of water.

The other member of the trio was Virbius, a shadowy figure in the Roman pantheon, who was either Diana's servant or her husband. He is thought to have been a reincarnation—his name means "twice a man"—of Hippolytus, the son of Theseus and Antiope. Hippolytus was wrongly accused of rape and cursed by his father. The sea god Poseidon responded to the curse by causing Hippolytus to fall from his chariot. He became entangled in the reins and was dragged to his death by his horses. Because of the way Hippolytus (Virbius) died, most scholars believe that horses were banned from the temple of Diana, although some have suggested that they were

used as sacrifices. With the exception of Virbius, men were denied entry to Diana's hallowed ground: the goddess had no interest in them, and they might have had a bad influence on women.

Above: In this 17th-century painting by Luca Giordano (1632–1705), Diana falls in love with the sleeping shepherd Endymion.

How Diana reached Italy

Most temples to Diana were built in groves of oak trees, which were particularly sacred to the goddess. The most famous, and possibly the first, shrine to her was at Aricia (modern Ariccia, Italy) in a grove on the shores of a lake known then as Speculum Dianae ("Diana's Mirror"), and now as Lake Nemi.

The exact date of the temple's foundation is unknown, but it was said to have been built in the aftermath of the Trojan War in the 12th or 13th century BCE. At the start of the conflict between Greece and Troy, Iphigeneia, the eldest daughter of Agamemnon, King of Troy, and his queen, Clytemnestra, had been offered as a sacrifice to the goddess Artemis. At the last minute, however, Artemis substituted a deer for Iphigeneia on the altar, and

transported the maiden to the land of the Taurians in the Cimmerian Chersonese (part of the Crimea, in modern Ukraine). There Iphigeneia served Artemis as a priestess, in which role she was required to sacrifice anyone who landed on the shores of the island. She carried out her duties until one day she recognized a newly arrived traveler as her long-lost brother, Orestes. Joyfully reunited, the pair plotted their escape. They killed King Thoas of the Chersonese and fled to Italy, where Orestes built a shrine at Aricia in thanksgiving for their deliverance. In time, the goddess who had inspired the shrine became known as Diana Nemorenis (Diana of the Woods) instead of Artemis.

This myth is important because it connects Diana with the earlier Greek deity, and it also indicates that human sacrifices were made to her. Although there is no firm evidence of such sacrifices, and although the Iphigeneia story could mean that Artemis/Diana was opposed to such practices, persistent rumors that sacrifices might have taken place both maintain Diana's mystique and cast a shadow over her reputation. Like Virbius, Diana is an ambivalent deity: fundamentally good, but with a hint of menace.

Another tradition that developed at Aricia was that of Rex Nemorensis or "King of the Grove." Historians believe that the figure may well have been a version of the Green Man, or forest spirit, a common figure in European mythology. Rex Nemorensis, who was supposedly a runaway slave or a fugitive, was the goddess's priest and guardian of the grove. He was obliged to reassert his right to his position annually by a ritual fight to the death with an opponent, who would challenge him by plucking a golden bough from the sacred oak. It is on this legendary ritual that Scottish anthropologist James Frazer based the title of his monumental book on comparative mythology *The Golden Bough* (1890–1915).

The golden bough was reputed to open the passageway to the underworld, and, as such, was sought by Aeneas for his descent in Book Six of the *Aeneid*, the epic poem by Virgil (70–19 BCE). The bough in question was mistletoe, a plant that grows on the oak, and was sacred to the druids, the priests of the ancient Celts.

The oak figures in Celtic lore as the Cosmic Tree, which marks the shaman's gateway to his trance. The Greek word for oak (*drys*) is related to the word for "door." (In Old Irish, both are called *dair*.) It is also related to the word for "tree." (The oak was believed to be the first tree.)

Diana in literature and art

In most works of art, Diana is depicted indulging in one of two main activities: consorting with a sisterhood of nymphs around pools and springs, or racing with them through the forest in pursuit of wild game. She often wears a short tunic that seductively exposes her legs or shoulders, and she carries a quiver of arrows on her back. She is usually accompanied by a hound or an antlered stag, her traditional familiars.

Such images are derived from several earlier legends of Artemis. In Asia Minor, for example, Artemis had been known as Lady of the Beasts, and was depicted giving birth to various wild animals. Animals play a large role in myths related to Artemis. When the hunter Actaeon surprised Diana and her nymphs while they were bathing, Artemis was so angered by his intrusion that she turned him into a stag, although his mind remained human. He fled into the forest, pursued by his wolflike hunting hounds, which eventually caught him and tore him to pieces.

The symbolism of this myth is complex, and obscure. Petroglyphs, carvings or inscriptions on rocks, dating from as early as the third millennium BCE document the hunter as animal-man, identified with and empowered by the spirits of particular animals. It is through these animal "friends" that the hunter attained the wild nature needed to guide him in the hunt. To kill the animal, the hunter needed to become totally familiar with its habits and to identify with its spirit. Ritual ceremonies ensured that the hunter would make a good kill, helped protect him from the potential anger of Nature, and sought the renewal and fertility of the

Right: This painting (1867) by Pierre-Auguste Renoir (1841–1919) depicts Diana the huntress with Actaeon in the form of a dead stag.

Above: This watercolor painting, Lake Nemi *(1818), is by English artist J. M. W. Turner (1775–1851).*

Other Temples to Diana

In addition to the shrine at Aricia, there were numerous other temples to Diana throughout the ancient Roman world. One of the most famous was built on Mount Tifata (modern Monte Maddaloni, north of the Italian town of Capua). The mountain's ancient name indicates that a grove of holm oaks once grew on it. This has led some commentators to conclude that, long before the mountain was taken over by followers of the goddess, it had been a cult sanctuary of the druids, whose name is derived from *drys*, the Greek word for their sacred oak tree.

According to legend, Mount Tifata was originally dedicated to Diana by the Roman dictator Egerius Baebius (or Laevius) of Tusculum, during the time of the Latin League, a confederation of various peoples of central Italy from the sixth to fourth century BCE. Partly in an effort to control this politico-religious movement, Servius Tullius, the sixth king of Rome (578–534 BCE), relocated the cult to Rome, where he established its new headquarters and decreed the construction of the specially designed Temple of Diana on Aventine Hill. In this poor area of the capital city, the main worshipers would have been the lower classes and female slaves. Female slaves were one of Diana's responsibilities: Diana was their patroness, and they could claim asylum in her temples. The festival of Diana was held every year on the Ides of August (August 13).

animal species. The hunter "begged permission" of the animal's spirit to be allowed to hunt it. Rituals such as these have been practiced by many hunting peoples through the ages, including Native Americans and Aborigines. Animals that served as guides, such as the horse, the wolf, and the bear (all of which have been associated with Diana), were not usually hunted, or if they were, they were objects of sacrificial offerings, as on occasion was the hunter.

Later, Diana figured in various occult practices. In alchemy she represented the conjunction of Luna and Sol, the moon and the sun. As goddess of the moon she was linked to Hecate, the patroness of black magic and witchcraft. According to Gnostic, or occult, Christian heresy, her "shining" persona as Lucina was divided from its opposite, darkness, to produce Lucifer, the devil.

CARL RUCK

Bibliography

Bulfinch, Thomas. *Bulfinch's Mythology.* New York: Modern Library, 1998.

Hamilton, Edith. *Mythology: Timeless Tales of Gods and Heroes.* New York: Warner Books, 1999.

SEE ALSO: Actaeon; Animals; Apollo; Artemis; Cycles; Endymion; Festivals; Jupiter; Nymphs; Pan; Rome; Virginity.

DIOMEDES

A king of Argos and a suitor of Helen, Diomedes played a crucial role in the Greek victory in the Trojan War. His importance was partly the result of his bravery as a warrior and partly the result of his cunning, a quality that he shared with his comrade Odysseus.

Diomedes' grandfather was Oeneus, king of the city of Calydon in central Greece. His father, Tydeus, was forced to flee Calydon after killing one of his relatives, possibly his uncle or brother. In Argos he married Deipyle, daughter of King Adrastus, who bore him Diomedes. Tydeus's fate mirrored that of Polyneices, the son of the Theban king Oedipus, who also left his homeland for Argos and married a daughter of Adrastus. Tydeus supported Polyneices in his attempt to seize the throne of Thebes from his brother, Eteocles, but the expedition was a disaster and both men died.

Early exploits

Like his father, Diomedes was a valiant fighter. Ten years after Tydeus's death, he joined a force known as the Epigoni (descendants), who vowed to succeed where their fathers had failed in Thebes. The Epigoni fulfilled their vow and installed Polyneices' son on the throne. Diomedes also sought vengeance for his father's exile from Calydon. He killed the cousins who had taken the throne from King Oeneus, and crowned Oeneus's son-in-law king. Yet Diomedes' greatest achievement as a fighter was in the Trojan War, the 10-year conflict between the

Greeks and the Trojans that began when the Trojan prince Paris abducted Helen, wife of the Greek king Menelaus. As one of Helen's many admirers, Diomedes had promised to defend the honor of anyone who married her, so he led a fleet of 80 ships to carry the Greek army to Troy.

The Trojan War

Diomedes was one of the greatest Greek champions in the Trojan War. In the *Iliad*, the poet Homer describes him as second only to Achilles, and makes frequent references to "Diomedes of the great war cry." In other versions, Diomedes is even braver than Achilles, whose petulant behavior when his slave girl Briseis is taken from him almost costs the Greeks victory.

Diomedes killed many Trojans in battle and, with the assistance of the goddess Athena, injured two deities. He wounded Aphrodite when she intervened to rescue her son, the Trojan hero Aeneas, from Diomedes' onslaught. In the same battle Diomedes fought Hector, Paris's brother and a favorite of Ares, the god of war. Athena helped Diomedes thrust his spear at Ares, wounding the god and causing him to flee the battle.

Diomedes' natural cunning and his partnership with Odysseus had an even more significant impact on the course of the war. Two episodes in particular illustrate the pair's capacity for deception. In one story they tricked the hermit Philoctetes out of his magic bow and arrows, which he had inherited from Heracles. The weapons allowed the Greeks to fulfill one prophecy of victory over

Left: This statue of Diomedes was carved by Polyclitus, one of the greatest Greek sculptors of the fifth century BCE.

Above: In this painting by Erasmus Quellinus (1607–1678), Odysseus and Diomedes give presents to the daughters of Lycomedes. One of the "girls" is Achilles in disguise; he gives himself away by seizing the weapons.

the Trojans. Diomedes and Odysseus fulfilled another when they stole the Palladium, a wooden statue to Athena, from inside Troy. Both the Greeks and the Trojans believed that, as long as the Palladium remained inside its walls, Troy was safe. However, disguised as beggars, the pair passed unnoticed into the city and stole the statue. These stories demonstrate the importance of sacred objects to the morale of the side that possessed them.

After the Trojan War

When Diomedes returned to Argos following the end of the Trojan War, he did not receive a hero's welcome, but discovered that his wife had been unfaithful in his absence and that his claim to the throne was disputed. Some writers suggest that this outcome was caused by the Greek prince Oeax, who believed that his brother Palamedes had been murdered by Diomedes and Odysseus. Accordingly, Oeax told Diomedes' wife that her husband was returning from Troy with a new lover. This legend may have inspired the

medieval story of Troilus and Cressida, later retold by Geoffrey Chaucer (c. 1342–1400) in a long poem and by William Shakespeare (1564–1616) in a play. In the former version, Troilus, son of the Trojan king Priam, falls in love with Cressida, only to be heartbroken when the Trojan woman switches her affections to Diomedes. Other Greek sources maintain that Diomedes' ill-fortune after the war was Aphrodite's punishment for the injury he had caused her. All the sources agree that Diomedes left Greece for Italy, but there are several different accounts of what he did there. Some state that he was killed by the king of Apulia; others that he founded several Italian cities, including Brindisi and Arpi. The Greek poet Pindar (c. 522–c. 438 BCE) even suggests that Athena made Diomedes a god.

ANDREW CAMPBELL

Bibliography

Bulfinch, Thomas. *Myths of Greece and Rome.* New York: Viking Penguin, Inc., 1998.

Homer, and Robert Fagles, trans. *The Iliad.* New York: Penguin USA, 2003.

SEE ALSO: Achilles; Aeneas; Aphrodite; Ares; Helen; Heracles; Menelaus; Odysseus; Priam; Troilus.

DIONYSUS

Dionysus was the Greek god of wine, and, among other things, vegetation and human emotion. Worshiped throughout the Hellenic world, he was particularly honored with a major festival in Athens. He was believed to be the resident god at Delphi during the winter months when Apollo was away.

Below: This Roman copy of a Greek marble sculpture of the fourth century BCE depicts Dionysus and a satyr.

Dionysus was the son of Zeus and Semele, a mortal daughter of Cadmus, King of Thebes. When Hera, the wife of Zeus, found out that Semele was pregnant with her husband's child, she was consumed with jealousy and devised a plot to destroy the girl. Disguising herself as an old nursemaid, she persuaded Semele to ask her lover to show himself to her in all his divine glory. When Zeus promised Semele he would grant all her wishes, she asked to see him as he appeared on Mount Olympus. Knowing in advance the frightful consequences of complying with this request, Zeus tried to deny Semele her wish, but she insisted. Zeus drew himself up to his full height, thunder echoed around him, and lightning flashed from his body. Semele was at once destroyed by the divine fire.

Born from his father's thigh

Zeus did not want his child to die with its mother, so he snatched the unborn baby from the ashes of Semele's body and sewed the child into his own thigh. In time, Zeus gave birth to his twice-born son. Dionysus was therefore known as the god of double birth, because he had been reborn from the body of Zeus. Although half mortal, Dionysus was made wholly divine from the time of his birth, because the mortality of his mother had been burned away in the flash of Zeus's lightning.

Hera's spite did not end there, however. She then ordered the Titans to eat the infant Dionysus. The Titans were an older generation of gods who had been defeated in battle and replaced by Zeus and the Olympians. They

413

tore Dionysus limb from limb and had just started to cook him when Rhea, a Titan and fertility goddess, intervened and hid him, disguised as a girl, at the court of Athamas, king of Orchomenus in Greece. Hera then drove Athamas mad, so Dionysus had to find refuge elsewhere. He was eventually raised by mountain nymphs in Phrygia, a remote area of Asia Minor (part of modern Turkey), and later moved to eastern Thrace, another isolated region that bounds the Hellespont (the modern Dardanelles, the straits between the Aegean and the Black Sea).

This distance from civilization is crucial to the cult of Dionysus—he represented, more than anything, submission to the urge to "let oneself go," and to behave in a way that would be embarrassing if anyone else were watching. That explains his association with wine, an alcoholic drink that reduces inhibitions.

Once Dionysus had established his rites in this farflung corner of the Hellenic world, he brought them to the heart of Greece. Yet his cult always remained to some extent furtive, and he was generally worshiped in wild fields, mountains, and other remote places, away from the cities.

Dionysus and Art

Dionysus is a shadowy, ambivalent god whose followers flirt with drunkenness, insanity, and death. Because of the association between creativity and the abandonment of self-control, Dionysus has been attractive to artists through the ages. He is usually depicted as a bearded youth, wearing a crown of vines with grapes. Often he holds the *thyrsos*, a wand that is a fertility symbol, and a cup of wine. He is often accompanied by maenads (female acolytes) and goatlike deities—usually satyrs, but sometimes Silenus or the pipe-playing Pan.

Images of Dionysus are common on classical Greek vases. In Renaissance European art, Dionysus became more or less interchangeable with Bacchus, his Roman equivalent. Among the best-known depictions of Dionysus or Bacchus are by Michelangelo (1475–1564), Titian (c. 1489–1576), Caravaggio (1573–1610), Peter Paul Rubens (1577–1640), Nicolas Poussin (1594–1665), and Diego Velázquez (1599–1660).

Below: Bacchus and Ariadne *was painted from 1523 to 1524 by Titian, an artist of the Italian Venetian school.*

Women in particular followed him and his rituals, for thus they could escape from their domestic duties and live at one with nature. In time men too joined in these rites.

Honoring Dionysus

The followers of Dionysus were said to have many extraordinary powers. They could make fountains of water, milk, and wine spring from the earth. They could not be harmed by fire, which they carried in their hands or on their heads. The priest and other prominent worshipers would also carry a *thyrsos*, an ivy-twined wooden rod or staff tipped with a pinecone.

Celebrations in honor of Dionysus varied from time to time, but they would often involve hunting. Any wild animal that was caught would be torn apart with bare hands (a deed called *sparagmos*). Its blood would then be drunk, and its flesh eaten raw (a ritual known as *omophagia*). Through these rites it was thought the participants could become one with nature and take the god within them.

As a god of nature, Dionysus looked after the earth while Apollo (the sun god) was away for the winter;

Above: This illustration from a 17th-century edition of Ovid's Metamorphoses *shows Dionysus turning pirates into dolphins.*

Dionysus was responsible for bringing the crops back to life each spring. He represented such natural forces as the sap which rises in the trees and brings out their leaves; he caused the flowers to bloom and the fruits to come from them. Dionysus also inspired animals to mate and bring forth their young. When plants died off in the fall, people prayed to Dionysus that he would return nature to its bloom in the spring, and when the plants reappeared they thanked him for restoring nature.

God of wine

One of the plants Dionysus especially cared for was the grapevine, the source of wine. We are told that he taught the art of winemaking to an Athenian farmer named Icarius. When Icarius shared his new drink with his fellow farmers, they thought he had poisoned them and killed him. His daughter Erigone looked for him everywhere in vain until her dog Maera led her to her father's grave. In

despair she hanged herself, while Maera jumped into a well and drowned. Dionysus was so angry at these events that he drove all Athenian girls mad, causing them to hang themselves as well. Finally, an annual festival for Dionysus was established at the time of the wine harvest. As part of the ceremonies young girls would swing on suspended ropes with platforms—according to legend, this was the invention of the swing.

Dionysus was also the god of human emotion. While Apollo represented thought and rational action, Dionysus cared for the opposite elements of the human soul—instinct and self-indulgence. Excitement and any feeling of freedom are inspired by this god.

Adventures of Dionysus

There are many legends associated with Dionysus. One story reports how he was once kidnapped by pirates. As they sailed over the seas, Dionysus suddenly revealed his true identity, causing a grapevine to grow from the ship's mast and a bear to appear suddenly on deck. He then turned himself into a lion. The terrified pirates jumped into the sea, but they did not drown: Dionysus changed them into dolphins. That is why dolphins are always friendly to humans, because they were once human themselves.

Another story of Dionysus is that he cared for Ariadne, a mortal princess who helped Theseus after he had slain the Minotaur in Crete. The thoughtless hero then abandoned her on the island of Naxos. Dionysus saw the frightened maiden on the shore and swept down to rescue her. He took her up to Mount Olympus and married her. He later changed her wedding crown into the constellation Corona Borealis.

The fate of those who denied Dionysus

Because Dionysus touched the mind in a special way, when he was angered by those who ignored him, he drove them mad. When he was honored, Dionysus was a most gentle god, but when dishonored, he was one of the most terrible divinities in the pantheon. To the Greeks, therefore, the crucial fact about Dionysus was that those who submitted to him—in other words, acknowledged the wild side of their own nature—would be rewarded with joy, while those who denied his power would be punished. Many stories show the god's vengefulness and extreme brutality to the impious. The most famous of these legends is set in Thebes. When Dionysus returned to the city in which he had been conceived, King Pentheus refused to honor him and tried to imprison him. Dionysus took swift revenge on the king and his city. First, he drove all the Theban women mad, sending them to the mountains as maenads, and made Agave, Pentheus's mother, their leader. Then Dionysus slowly maddened Pentheus as well. Persuading him to dress as a woman, he led the king to the mountains. There the women saw him spying on them from a pine tree and rushed to destroy him. Agave herself pulled down the tree and tore him apart with her bare hands. All the women joined in the violence. Thus Pentheus died for denying Dionysus. The god then restored Agave to sanity and made her realize what she had done. Agave had to go into exile forever, knowing that she had killed her own son.

Dionysus is also central to the myth of Hephaestus, god of fire and metalwork, who, having been thrown off Mount Olympus, landed on the island of Lemnos. There he stayed, unforgiven by his parents, Zeus and Hera. In time, however, the king and queen of the gods realized that they needed Hephaestus. So Dionysus descended to Lemnos, made the fire god drunk with wine, and led him back up to Olympus, where he was reconciled with his parents. Hephaestus then married Aphrodite, the goddess of love, and built for her a beautiful home with robots to do all the housework.

The Dionysia

A five-day festival known as the City Dionysia was held in Athens between the first quarter and the full moon of March (usually March 24–28). The festival marked the end of winter (the Dionysian part of the year) and the start of spring, the resurgence of Indestructible Life (Zöe).

The Dionysia began when a wooden image of Dionysus was taken from his principal temple in the city and replaced on the *eskhara* (hearth) of the temple near the Academy. There would be a ceremony comprising hymns and the sacrifice of a male goat to Dionysus. Following that ritual, there was a banquet and wine from the god. Then every morning for the next three days, three tragedies would be performed. These plays were based on myths known to every Greek, but each playwright told the familiar story in a different way. After the main event, a short and rowdy entertainment, called a satyr play, was staged. This cartoon-like retelling of another famous myth was intended to bring the audience out of the fear aroused by the tragedies, and prepare them for the comedy that evening. On the last day of the festival, judges awarded first, second, and third prizes to the playwrights whose tragedies had been performed.

Right: This vase, with an engraved image of Dionysus reclining on a couch during the grape harvest, was excavated at Pompeii, Italy.

417

Above: The theater of Dionysus on the hillside below the Acropolis in central Athens, Greece. Some of the most important plays in history were first performed in the amphitheater.

The rituals practiced by the Greeks for Dionysus were known as *orgia,* meaning "holy ceremonies." The followers of the god, the maenads, who as a group were called a *thiasos,* went to the mountains wearing unbelted robes and wearing crowns of ivy (some vase paintings also show crowns of snakes). They carried the *thyrsos,* and tamborines and drums to make music. They would dance wildly, then rush upon an animal to sacrifice it to the god. There was no priest or priestess to kill the victim, but the maenads themselves would tear the animal apart, drink its warm blood, and eat its raw flesh. By these rites they would become one with Dionysus.

Although many of the celebrations of Dionysus took place in remote locations, the most famous annual celebration of the god was held on the south slope of the Acropolis, in the center of Athens. This was the City Dionysia, a drama festival that was put on each spring. During this five-day event both tragedies and comedies were performed in a theater dedicated especially to the god. It was here that the plays of famous Greek dramatists, such as Sophocles, Aeschylus, Euripides, and Aristophanes were first acted out—three tragedies in the morning, and a comedy in the evening. Although few of the plays were about Dionysus himself, they were all put on in his honor.

Dionysus in art

It was believed that when he set foot on earth, Dionysus was usually accompanied by small bands of satyrs. These creatures—half man, half goat—enjoyed drinking, chasing nymphs, and generally leading a wild, dissolute life. Many vase paintings from ancient Greece show the god with his crown of ivy, holding his *thyrsos,* and surrounded by attendant dancing satyrs.

Dionysus is the god most frequently shown in ancient art. Perhaps this is because he represents so many aspects of our world, including the plants that arise from the earth each spring, and the emotions of joy and excitement we all feel.

KARELISA HARTIGAN

Bibliography

Bulfinch, Thomas. *Myths of Greece and Rome.* New York: Viking Penguin, Inc., 1998.

Howatson, M.C., and Ian Chilvers. *Concise Oxford Companion to Classical Literature.* New York: Oxford University Press, 1993.

SEE ALSO: Aphrodite; Cadmus; Hephaestus; Hera; Maenads; Theseus; Titans; Zeus.

DIS

Although there are few myths about Dis, and little evidence that he was widely worshiped, he remains one of the most important gods in the Roman pantheon because of his dual role as the god of death and the lord of the underworld.

The Romans identified Dis with the Greek god Pluton (Latin: Pluto), which is an alternative name for Hades. Hades was both the god of the underworld and the underworld itself. Dis was also equated with the pagan Italian god Orcus, and was at times identified with Soranus, a god of the Sabines, an ancient people who lived to the northeast of Rome. The name Dis is originally a contracted form of *dives*, the Latin for "riches," just as the name Pluton (or Plouton) is derived from the Greek word for "rich": *ploutos*. The element of "riches" in the names Dis and Pluto could suggest that Dis was originally a god of the fields, responsible for the wealth of the crops, which were sent up from underneath the earth. Alternatively, it might indicate that Dis is to be understood as a collector (rather than a giver) of wealth, since everyone who dies goes to Hades, often taking various valuables with them in their graves.

Dis as Hades

Although there are no known myths of Dis himself, Hades is so closely associated with him that the same stories are equally applicable to both deities. Hades, Zeus, and Poseidon were the sons of Cronus and Rhea. When Zeus ousted his

Below: The Last Judgment *(1541), by Italian painter Michelangelo (1475–1564), depicts the arrival of damned souls in the underworld.*

The Last Judgment

The idea of someone being judged after death on the life they have led on earth is an old one, predating Christianity. Romans believed in such a judgment, as murals painted in the tomb of a Sabine priest, Vincentius, and his wife, Vibia, demonstrate. Three murals, with explanatory inscriptions, depict the anticipated afterlife adventures of Vibia.

The first mural depicts Pluto carrying Vibia to the underworld in his four-horse chariot. In the second mural, Vibia appears in the company of Alcestis. In the same mural Mercury leads the two women toward the middle of the scene, where the lord of the underworld, Dispater ("Dis the father"), sits on a raised platform with Aeracura. Dispater stretches out his right hand toward a group of three goddesses, the Divine Fates. (In mythology, the Fates determine the length of human lives.)

This second mural has the solemn character of a judgment scene. Alcestis appears to be present as a character witness for Vibia, to testify that Vibia was as virtuous as she herself had been.

In the third mural, a "good angel" (*angelus bonus*) leads Vibia to a celestial banquet, where she sits with the other guests. She no longer wears her cloak over her head as in the previous scenes, but instead wears a wreath. In the foreground, two young men appear to be playing some game, emphasizing the carelessness of the scene, and to the far right a large amphora (wine jar) reminds us that there is wine to drink in the afterlife. The party that Vibia has joined is identified by an inscription as "those who have been chosen by the judgment of the good."

father, the three children divided the realms: Hades received the underworld, Zeus the sky, and Poseidon the sea.

In some works of art, Hades is envisaged as the judge in the Last Judgment (see box, above). The most famous myth associated with Hades, however, is the story of his niece, Persephone, whom he abducted to the underworld to be his wife. Persephone's mother, Demeter, was overcome with grief at her loss, and searched the world for her until Zeus, who had originally authorized the kidnapping, took pity on her and sent his messenger, Hermes, down to the underworld to fetch Persephone back. Persephone, however, had eaten in the underworld and therefore could never leave it. Although she was allowed partial freedom, she had to return below the earth for four or six months of every year. Her return to earth each year coincided with the start of spring. Thus Hades represents the attempt to thwart annual renewal.

Worship

Unusual for a Roman deity, Dis is associated with very few cults. It was believed by the Romans that the only way that it was possible to communicate with Dis was through oaths and curses, which were generally frowned on and discouraged. People sacrificed black animals to him, and they were always careful to look away while performing the sacrifice. The most common shrines for Dis or Pluto were the so-called Plutonia, which were said to mark entrances to the underworld.

According to legend, the servants of a Sabine named Valesius miraculously discovered a marble altar inscribed to both Dis and Proserpina (Persephone) at the edge of the Campus Martius (Field of Mars) near the Roman capital city. They found it at a depth of 20 feet (6 m) while they were digging to lay the foundations for an altar, following instructions given in dreams to the children of Valesius. In historic times, this altar was used for sacrifices during the Ludi Saeculares (Secular Games), an event held every century to avert the plague. An altar found in Rome in 1886–1887 underneath the Palazzo Cesarini was for a long time wrongly identified as the legendary altar of Dis and Proserpina. The real location of the altar must have been near the Vittorio Emanuele II bridge over the Tiber River, where fragmentary records of the Ludi Saeculares were unearthed in the 20th century.

Art

In the art from ancient Greece, the god Hades, or Pluton, is represented as a bearded figure with a strong familiar resemblance to his brother Zeus. He is usually depicted holding a scepter or a cornucopia (horn of plenty). Pluton should not be confused with the boy Plutus (or Ploutos), son of Demeter and Iasion, who played a role in the myth of the Eleusinian Mysteries, and is also frequently shown holding a cornucopia. Dis is represented only rarely in Roman art. When he does appear, he is usually shown in the company of his consort Aeracura, who is a Persephone-like figure. Dis does not appear in later art, while Pluto appears only in scenes of the abduction of Persephone.

FEYO SCHUDDEBOOM

Bibliography
Bulfinch, Thomas. *Myths of Greece and Rome.* New York: Viking Penguin, Inc., 1998.
Howatson, M.C., and Ian Chilvers. *Concise Oxford Companion to Classical Literature.* New York: Oxford University Press, 1993.

SEE ALSO: Death and the Afterlife; Demeter; Fates; Hades; Persephone; Zeus.

DRAGONS

The dragon is the closest thing to a universal monster. Dragons are fantasy creatures, yet people all over the world have imagined them. However, there are significant differences among the attributes of these creatures. For example, the European dragon is usually seen as a figure of evil, while the Asian dragon is generally a figure of wisdom and strength.

The dragon bears a strong resemblance to many types of lizards. *Varanus komodoensis*, a member of the monitor lizard family native to Indonesia and the largest type of lizard in the world, gained its common name Komodo dragon because of its dragonlike appearance. Some scholars have suggested that legends and myths of dragons may have arisen as an explanation for ancient discoveries of prehistoric fossils. They remark on the fact that many fossils of large winged reptiles have been found recently in mainland China, leading to speculation that similar dragonlike fossils were also uncovered by the ancient Chinese. This might explain why dragons were an important element in ancient Chinese mythology.

Generally dragons are popularly thought of as reptilian quadrupeds (walking on four legs) or bipeds (walking on two legs), scaly, winged, and often fire breathing. In addition to their ability to fly and scorch, however, they are also often able to talk and, more important, to reason. Whether dragons are figures of good or of evil, they are almost always clever and resourceful.

Dragons in creation myths

The earliest creation myths from western Asia usually began with stories in which the world was formed either by a female reptile (variously termed a snake or a dragon) or from her body. The Babylonian epic *Enuma Elish*, which

Above: The dragons on this item of Vietnamese furniture are symbols of imperial power. They guard the yin-and-yang pearl of inner energy.

was composed around 1900 BCE, relates how the god Marduk created the earth out of the body of the monster-dragon Tiamat, who was the mother of all the gods.

In Hittite myth the dragon Illuyanka battled the storm god and stole his eye and heart, but ultimately the god prevailed and crushed the serpent, an act celebrated as part of the Hittites' annual New Year ceremony.

In Greek myth Typhon and his mate Echidna were the serpent children of Gaia and Tartarus; Zeus slew Typhon, but Echidna lived on to protect her own children: the Nemean Lion, the Hydra (a poisonous, many-headed snake), Cerberus (a three-headed dog with a snake's tail), Ladon (a snake with a hundred heads), the Chimera (a three-headed monster), and the Sphinx (a monster with the head of woman, the body of a lion, and the wings of a bird), all of which were defeated by human heroes.

In the Rig Veda, the sacred text of the Hindus, the warrior god Indra defeated the dragon Vritra, who had swallowed all the waters of the world, hoarding them in his fortress like treasure. Indra's story is similar to that of the Iranian god Verethraghna, who slew a dragon and freed the flow of water.

These stories introduce a number of themes that persist in most dragon myths. Dragons are associated with water, either living in water, embodying water, or stealing water. They also live in caves, either under the earth or under the water. In other words, dragons belong to the underworld. They represent forces that spring from out of the earth and, in psychological terms, unconscious desires. Yet dragons also fly and breathe fire, which make them able to function in all four of the primary elements: earth, air, fire, and water.

Heroes battling dragons

Dragons are thieves, stealing and hoarding treasure, which might be gold and jewels or pretty young girls. Dragons are also often the main adversaries for heroes. Gods, demigods, heroes, and saints all battle dragons. In the opinion of many folklorists, the tale type known as dragon slayer is the archetypal folk tale, and in the opinion of many mythologists, the defeat of a dragon is the archetypal way in which an Indo-European hero demonstrates his heroism. This means that what heroes do is slay dragons; what dragons exist for is to be slain by heroes.

Sometimes the hero slays the dragon in straightforward battle, succeeding by sheer might. The success of these heroes, such as Saint George (see box, page 423) or Beowulf, illustrates their spiritual worth because of their physical prowess. Other dragon slayers, however, prevail by trickery, such as Sir John Lambton, who slew the Lambton Worm by wearing a coat of razor-plated armor that cut the dragon to pieces (see box, page 424). In such cases the hero out-tricks the cunning dragon, besting him mentally as well as physically.

Many gods and heroes from ancient Greek mythology also battle dragons. For example, Apollo, the god associated with the sun and rationality, battled the dragon Python to take over the sanctuary at Delphi. Python guarded an oracle of Themis, a Titan whose name means "law" and

Left: Symbolically, dragons and snakes are closely related. Both were called "worm" in ancient Indo-European myths.

Saint George and the Dragon

The historical Saint George was probably a Roman soldier martyred in Palestine around 303 CE. His early cult focused on his martyrdom, but about one thousand years after his death, the story of his defeat of a dragon was published in Jacobus de Voragine's *Legenda aurea* ("Golden Legend"; 13th century). George is said to have come across a pagan city near Silena in Libya which was being terrorized by a dragon that lived in a lake. The citizens gave the dragon two sheep a day to eat, but when they ran out of sheep, they began offering human sacrifices chosen by lot. When George arrived, the lot had fallen upon the king's daughter. George promised to kill the dragon if the people would convert to Christianity. He pierced the dragon with his spear, led it to the city with the princess's belt, and then beheaded the dragon before the city's population. Fifteen thousand people are said to have converted as a result.

Before the legend was published, it was extremely popular during the Crusades, when a vision of Saint George before the capture of Antioch in 1098 was taken as an omen of victory. By the 13th century he was regarded as the patron saint of England; his feast day (April 23) was made a holiday in 1222. By saving the princess from the dragon, the soldier-saint came to be regarded as an important role model for chivalrous knights, who did battle in honor of their lady.

Below: This early-16th-century painting by Raphael depicts Saint George slaying the dragon in order to save the princess (right).

Above: This early-15th-century panel painting was originally made for the city of Padua in northern Italy. In medieval Europe the dragon was seen as a devilish creature, but some dynastic families, cities, and kingdoms adopted the dragon symbol as a show of power and authority.

The Lambton Worm

One of the best-known British dragon legends is that of the Lambton Worm, a beast that devastated Fatfield, in northeastern England, during the Middle Ages. One morning John Lambton went fishing in the River Wear, but all he caught was an eel-like creature that oozed black slime. A mysterious passerby warned him to destroy the worm as quickly as possible, but instead Lambton tossed it into a nearby well. Lambton soon went off on the Crusades. While he was gone, the worm grew ever larger until one day it emerged from the well and began to lay waste to the countryside. When Lambton returned from the wars, he vowed to destroy the worm. A wise woman advised him to make a suit of armor covered with razors so that when the dragon attempted to swallow him, it would be cut up into tiny pieces. However, she made him swear that he would kill the first living thing he met after he had killed the dragon. Failure to do so meant that there would be a curse on his descendants for nine generations. Lambton heeded the woman's advice and his suit of razors killed the dragon. Afterward the first living thing he saw was his father. Lambton could not kill him and the curse followed his family for the prescribed nine generations.

who embodied the customary divine order of the cosmos. The enmity of Apollo and Python predated Apollo's birth, for according to some sources Hera sent Python to kill Leto while she was pregnant with Apollo and Artemis. Apollo went after Python as soon as he was old enough to shoot a bow and arrow and killed him, taking over the oracle for himself.

The priestess who delivered the oracles was known as the Pythia, but her words had to be interpreted by priests of Apollo before being delivered to the questioner. Some scientists have suggested that the source of the Pythia's inspirational trances may have been some kind of hallucinogenic gas emitted through the volcanic fissures or seismic fault lines running under the oracle site. Although this theory cannot be proved, the concept of noxious fumes emerging from underground fits in with the mythology of the dragon.

The Greek myth of Perseus and Andromeda is another famous example of a hero defeating a dragon. Andromeda was the daughter of Cepheus, king of the Ethiopians. When his wife, Cassiopeia, boasted that she was more beautiful than the sea nymphs, they were deeply offended and complained to Poseidon, the sea god. He sent a flood and a sea monster to avenge them. An oracle told Cepheus that

Right: This is a 16th-century miniature painting of a mythical Ottoman knight battling a dragon.

he would only be able to get rid of the dragon if he sacrificed his daughter. Andromeda was chained to a rock on the seashore and left for the dragon. At this critical moment the hero Perseus flew by on his winged sandals and fell in love with her. Cepheus agreed that he could have her hand in marriage if he killed the dragon. Perseus killed the dragon by flying up—either on his winged sandals or on a winged horse, depending on the version— and attacking it from above with his sword. He set Andromeda free and the couple were married.

Heracles and the Hesperides

Heracles was the greatest of the Greek heroes. The goddess Hera inflicted madness upon him and he killed his children. Returned to sanity, he went to the Delphic Oracle to seek purification. He was told to serve the king of Tiryns and carry out all the tasks given him. Their successful completion would make him immortal.

The tasks became the famous 12 Labors of Heracles. One of them involved stealing the golden apples of the Hesperides. The Hesperides were singing nymphs who lived on an island at the far reaches of the earth. They guarded the tree bearing the golden apples, which was originally given as a wedding present to Zeus and Hera from Gaia, the earth mother. The garden was also watched over by Ladon, a hundred-headed dragon.

The bulk of Heracles' labor involved going from one source to another to find a way to defeat the dragon. Eventually he learned that only the Titan Atlas could pick the apples, so he tricked Atlas into carrying out the task for him. This is another example of someone defeating a dragon through trickery, although here the trick was played on someone else in order to get around the dragon.

Generally, the Greek dragons were not as mentally subtle as later Germanic and Celtic dragons, but rather something along the lines of giant reptilian guard dogs. They were not innately evil, merely ferocious. However, they were easily overcome by ingenuity or magic, and a hero was able to prove his bravery and skill by defeating or tricking them.

The death of Beowulf

In the Anglo-Saxon legend of Beowulf, the hero's final battle was with a dragon. A slave stole a cup from the dragon's hoard; the dragon laid waste to the countryside in retaliation. This Old English dragon lived within a burial

mound—an artificial cavern within the earth—and hoarded gold, which he protected by breathing out flames. Beowulf was forced to fight the dragon as one might put down a rabid dog. As long as the dragon stayed quietly on his hoard, he was allowed to live in peace, but when he began destroying the community, he had to be killed. In the myth, Beowulf was the king of the Geats and the only warrior brave enough to face the dragon; in fact, he was deserted by all his men but one. Although he killed the dragon by splitting open its soft underbelly, he himself was killed by the dragon's venom.

In Old Norse mythology, Fafnir was one of the most famous dragons, but he began life as a human. Fafnir and his brothers Regin and Otr were the sons of Hreidmar. The gods Odin, Loki, and Hénir killed Otr and paid his *weregild* (a fine for murder based on the social status of the victim) with cursed gold tricked out of the dwarf Andvari. Fafnir killed his father and took the treasure for himself. It was his possessiveness that caused him to turn into a dragon.

Years later, Regin induced the hero Sigurd to kill Fafnir so that Regin could get the gold himself. However, the method he suggested for killing the dragon (piercing his soft underbelly from below) would have killed Sigurd as well; Sigurd was warned of this by a mysterious stranger who turned out to be Odin. Odin also advised him how to survive the fatal dragon's blood that would spurt from Fafnir's wound.

As he died, Fafnir exchanged cryptic comments with Sigurd, warning him that he would be betrayed by Regin. When Sigurd roasted Fafnir's heart for Regin to eat, he accidentally drank some of the dragon's blood. It gave him the ability to understand the language of birds. The first bird conversation he overheard revealed that Regin intended to kill him. Sigurd therefore cut off Regin's head and took the treasure for himself. Advised by the birds, he set off in search of a fair maiden to wed.

Armies from Dragon's Teeth

A guardian dragon kept watch over the Golden Fleece, the object of a quest by the Greek hero Jason. Jason eventually found the fleece in Colchis, the land of King Aeetes. In order to acquire this treasure, Aeetes demanded that Jason sow dragons' teeth in a field; these teeth immediately turned into a ferocious army that Jason tricked into fighting each other by throwing a stone in their midst. To trick the guardian dragon, Jason enlisted the help of the witch Medea, the daughter of Aeetes. She charmed the dragon to sleep so that Jason could snatch the Golden Fleece.

The trick of throwing a stone into the midst of an army sprung up from sown dragon's teeth also occurs in a version of the story of Cadmus's founding of Thebes. The Theban dragon guarded the Stream of Ares. In this case, only five of the dragon army survived the battle, and they became the ancestors of the noble Theban families. Cadmus later married Harmonia, the daughter of Ares and Aphrodite. In their old age, Cadmus and Harmonia were turned into serpents.

Below: The scene depicted here is the battle among the soldiers who grew from the teeth of the dragon that Cadmus (left) had killed.

The Welsh Dragon

In his *Historia regum Britanniae* ("History of the Kings of Britain," c. 1136), Geoffrey of Monmouth included the story of the tyrant Vortigern's repeated attempts to build a castle at Dinas Emrys in Wales. Each time, the foundations were mysteriously swallowed by the earth during the night. He called his magicians, who advised him to find a child who never had a father, kill him, and sprinkle his blood over the foundation stones. The boy Merlin was discovered to have been fathered by a demon, and he was brought to Vortigern to be sacrificed. Merlin, however, proceeded to show that the foundations sank because, underneath the building site, there was a pond. When the pond was drained, Vortigern and Merlin discovered two hollow stones; when the stones were broken open, two dragons—one red, one white—emerged and began fighting, flying through the air and breathing fire.

At first the white dragon appeared to be winning, but then the red dragon prevailed. Merlin interpreted this for Vortigern as meaning that the Saxons, represented by the white dragon, would appear to conquer Britain, but the Welsh, represented by the red dragon, would avenge themselves. The red dragon became the emblem of Wales and is still found on the Welsh flag. Like many dragons, those in this story are associated with water and found underground. They also show similarities to Asian dragons in that they are associated with earth energies and kingship.

Above: The red dragon on the Welsh flag symbolizes victory and relates to the myth that the Welsh red dragon defeated the Saxon white dragon.

Asian dragons

Asian dragons were much more positive figures than European dragons. Chinese and Japanese dragons, for example, were symbols of imperial power. In many cases they were said to have mated with humans, the offspring of the union becoming great rulers. In contrast, European dragons' sexual advances toward humans were viewed as threatening and dangerous. The dragon became a symbol of the emperor and appeared on the Chinese flag. During the Ch'ing dynasty (1644–1912) everything connected to

the emperor was described in terms of dragons: for example, the dragon throne, the dragon boat, and the dragon bed.

While Asian dragons were believed to control water—rain as well as bodies of water such as rivers, lakes, and seas—they were also associated with earth, especially mountains. The Chinese tradition of feng shui, a belief that is recognized in many parts of the world, is based on the idea that there are paths of energy flowing over and through the earth. These energy paths are visualized as dragon veins, and indeed the earth itself is seen as a living, benevolent dragon. There are three types of dragon veins: youthful veins are high ranges with jagged peaks; mature veins are lower with rounded peaks and gentle slopes; and old veins are lower still with small peaks and rugged slopes. The strongest energy is carried in the young veins, the energy in mature veins is more stable, and the energy in old veins is weak.

A Chinese creation myth

Chinese dragons also represented yang, or male energy. According to the *Shan Hai Ching*, a Chinese text written between the third century BCE and the early first century CE, an enormous red dragon with a human face lived in the northwestern desert where the sun did not shine. The opening and closing of his eyes created day and night, and

Below: The Nine Dragon Wall, of which this is a detail, is in Beihai Park, Beijing. The wall was built in 1756 and is made up of 424 large ceramic tiles. It includes 635 different dragons.

his breath made the winds and rain and summer and winter. Dragons were associated with the four cardinal directions, and some guarded treasure, governed the waters and the rain, and supported and protected the mansions of the gods in the sky. Japanese dragons shared the watery associations of Chinese dragons, living in lakes and governing the rains, but they were more likely to be vengeful and to have a taste for human sacrifice.

In Vietnamese mythology, the Dragon King (known as Long Vuong or Thuy-tl) was the ruler of waters, although he confined himself to the seas and delegated the fresh waters to his subordinates. He was a benevolent deity who often hired humans to build his palaces and paid them in pearls. When his children, roaming the world in the guise of aquatic animals or fish, were released by good-hearted fishers, they begged their father to reward their saviors with items of wealth or magic. These children sometimes married humans, bringing them wealth and success. The Dragon King's administrators, however, were not so kind. They could cause disasters, such as floods.

Above: *Perseus, who had been given the gift of flight from the gods, flies above the dragon that is threatening to devour the imprisoned Andromeda (right) in order to slay the creature. This painting (1602) is by Italian artist Giuseppe Cesari (c. 1568–1640).*

Left: This large bronze casting of a dragon stands in the Summer Palace in Beijing, China. The dragon represented the Chinese emperor's celestial powers and authority.

Serpent creatures

There are many other mythological beasts, such as the Indian nagas, the Rainbow Serpent of the Australian Aborigines, the African Damballah Ouedo, and the Norse serpents Jörmungand and Nidhogr, which have dragon characteristics but are closer to serpents. The imagery of serpents differs from dragons in that their ability to shed their skin is usually seen as representing death and rebirth. However, in Judeo-Christian cultures, dragons and serpents are often seen as equally evil; the mental acuity of the dragon is comparable to the subtlety of the serpent seducing the biblical Eve into taking the apple from the Tree of Knowledge.

Dragons also overlap with mythological sea serpents in many ways due to the dragon's association with water. Some argue that the monster defeated by Perseus was more of a sea serpent than a dragon. It had no desire for treasure, it did not guard anything, and it did not govern the waters in any way.

Despite the differences between European and Asian dragons, the persistence of their association with water, whether it is lakes, seas, rivers, rain clouds, or wells, is striking, as is their association with wisdom, whether it is perceived as being evil or benevolent wisdom. Another common characteristic is the dragon's frightening gaze. The word *dragon* comes from an ancient Greek word meaning "to see."

It is hard to determine whether the concept of the dragon arose in one place and spread throughout the Eurasian landmass (monogenesis) or if it arose in many different places at different times (polygenesis). The fact that beliefs in dragonlike serpents in many parts of the world associate these beasts with water suggests that there is some underlying universal symbolism.

LESLIE ELLEN JONES

Bibliography

Bates, Roy. *Chinese Dragons.* New York: Oxford University Press, 2002.

Bulfinch, Thomas. *Myths of Greece and Rome.* New York: Viking Penguin. Inc., 1998.

Shuker, Karl P. *Dragons: A Natural History.* New York: Simon and Schuster, 1995.

SEE ALSO: Andromeda; Cadmus; China; Demigods and Heroes; Heracles; Jason; Perseus; Southeast Asia; Tiamat; Typhon.

INDEX

Page numbers in *italics* refer to picture captions. Page numbers in **bold** refer to main articles.